D1579891

FLODDEN

To Cara

FLODDEN

NIALL BARR

TEMPUS

First published 2001
This edition first published 2003

Tempus Publishing Limited
The Mill, Brimscombe Port,
Stroud, Gloucestershire, GL5 2QG

British Library Cataloguing in Publication Data.
A catalogue record for this book is available from the British Library.

ISBN 0 7524 2593 5

Typesetting and origination by Tempus Publishing Limited
Printed in Great Britain by Midway Colour Print, Wiltshire

CONTENTS

ACKNOWLEDGEMENTS

The seeds for this book were planted when I was asked to take the staff of Army Headquarters, Scotland on a battlefield tour of a famous British battle. I would like to thank all of the staff at Craigiehall for their kindness, in particular Lt-Col. Valerie Hall and Col. Hugh Willing for their support. The staff of the Central Library, Royal Military Academy Sandhurst, and the library of the Joint Services Command and Staff College deserve many thanks for their unfailing ability to procure the most arcane of sources. The staff of the National Army Museum archives and the British Library are also deserving of praise for their quiet efficiency and assistance.

I would like to thank Geoffrey Wheeler for his expertise and detailed eye in providing the images in the book and Jonathan Reeve, at Tempus Publishing, for his patience and advice which has helped bring this project to fruition. Numerous colleagues have been helpful with my research and I would particularly like to thank my friends Gordon Connell, Grant Elliott, Gary Sheffield and Warren Chin for reading the manuscript. Needless to say, any errors or omissions are mine alone.

This book is dedicated to my wife, Cara Brandi, for her unfailing support and enthusiasm. She has made the steep climb up Piper's Hill to the Flodden memorial as many times as I have and I thank her for travelling with me every step of the way.

PREFACE

Today, we envisage clashes between England and Scotland as games 'fought' between teams of fifteen men on the rugby 'fields' of Murrayfield or Twickenham. These matches are deeply felt expressions of national loyalty and result in corresponding anguish or triumph at the final whistle. They are attended with all the trappings of ritual and ceremonial 'warfare'- the opposing teams 'fight' face-to-face and hand-to-hand in what appears to replicate the closeness of medieval combat. Scotland's new 'national anthem', *Flower of Scotland*, which is sung before these matches, derives its inspiration from the battle of Bannockburn. Yet in rehearsing Scotland and England's past, as fans at rugby matches are wont to do, the song's title is inevitably linked to the haunting lilt of *The Flowers of the Forest* and Scotland's greatest defeat at Flodden. With a capacity of 67,255, it is perhaps ironic that the stadium at Murrayfield can today hold far more people than fought on both sides at Bannockburn or Flodden.

The battle of Flodden has appalled and fascinated people for generations. The disastrous outcome which saw the king of Scots and the vast majority of his nobles wiped out in a single afternoon seems to mark a watershed in the affairs of Scotland and England. Writers and historians have inevitably contrasted the 'golden age' of James IV with the descent into violence and civil war in Scotland after 1514. The campaign of 1513 was certainly the last time that a king of Scotland led a united and powerful Scottish national army, based on the old feudal system, into battle. Less than one hundred years later, James VI of Scotland assumed the throne of England as James I in 1603, ending centuries of conflict between the two kingdoms. Yet the importance and significance of these contrasts and watersheds can be over-emphasised. Illness prevented James V from leading his army over the Solway Firth in 1542 and Pinkie, fought in 1547, represented the last battle between England and Scotland as independent kingdoms. Nonetheless, the dramatic events of Flodden appear to lie on the cusp of the new Renaissance understanding of the past, the profound military developments of the sixteenth century and the trauma of the Reformation. For all of these reasons, Flodden remains a landmark on our national consciousness.

Flodden remains endlessly fascinating for another reason. Anyone wishing to understand the events of 1513 has to rely on a limited number of sources, patchy official documents, ballads, poems and chronicles which inevitably leave gaps in our knowledge, questions unanswered, and room for interpretation and speculation. The fact is that there are only three versions of the battle which might claim the authenticity of eyewitness accounts. The brief *Articules of the Bataille*[1] was probably written by Thomas Howard, the Lord Admiral, while *The Trewe Encountre*[2] and Edward Hall's *The Triumphant Reigne of Kyng Henry VIII*[3] also seem to be based on eyewitness observation. Thomas Ruthal, Bishop of Durham, while not actually present, wrote two letters to Almoner Wolsey, which were based on reports by men who had fought at the battle.[4] It is certainly true that there are many more contemporary English accounts of the battle than Scottish ones. This is not surprising given the fact that virtually no Scotsman of note who witnessed the battle survived to tell the tale. There are no corresponding Scottish contemporary records to tell us the details of the 1513 campaign from the Scottish point of view. Thus any examination of Flodden has to be constructed from the available sources and from scanty evidence.

However, recent scholarship on James IV's reign,[5] particularly that undertaken by Dr Norman MacDougall,[6] has offered a much more realistic vision of James IV and Scotland in 1513. This book owes a great intellectual debt to these works. An understanding of the realities of sixteenth-century statecraft, and the deadly serious intent which was masked by chivalric pleasantries, suggests an entirely different picture of the events leading up to the Scottish invasion of England on 22 August 1513. Evidence concerning the Swiss military techniques emulated by the Scots can considerably advance our understanding of the deployment and nature of the battle, just as data drawn from the succeeding two centuries' use of gunpowder artillery can help to finally explain the nature of the first artillery duel in Britain. Knowledge of the wider European military developments and the capabilities of weaponry used at Flodden allow a sounder perception of what was militarily possible - what A.H. Burne called 'Inherent Military Probability'.[7] Just as importantly, modern understanding of men's behaviour in battle first explored by

Ardant du Picq,[8] and later by John Keegan,[9] can tell us much about the grim story related by the contemporary observers. By drawing evidence and information from as many related fields as possible, it is possible to build a convincing picture of this terrible battle.

1

A WEB OF INTRIGUE

On 11 August 1513, Lyon King-at-Arms, Herald of Scotland, arrived at the sumptuous camp of King Henry VIII of England, just outside the French town of Thérouanne. Lyon Herald:

> being almost dismayed seeing the King so nobly accompanied, with few words and meet good reverence delivered a letter to the King who received the letter and read it himself.[1]

The letter, from James IV, king of Scots, did not take the form of an open declaration of war, but rather an ultimatum. James demanded that Henry:

> desist from further invasion and utter destruction of our brother and cousin the Most Christian King★, to whom... we are bounden and obliged for mutual defence the one of the other, like as you and your confederates be obliged for mutual invasions and actual war; certifying you we will take

---

★ Honorific title of the king of France, Louis XII.

part in defence of our brother and cousin the Most Christian
King. And we will do what thing we trust may cause you to
desist from pursuit of him.[2]

Of course, by the time Lyon Herald delivered the letter to
Henry, Scottish preparations for war were well in hand.
Henry, aware that the northern counties of his kingdom
were now exposed to invasion while the main military force
of England was deployed in France, lost his temper. He
shouted at Lyon Herald that, 'I am the very owner of
Scotland, he holdeth it of me by homage,'[3] in a revival of the
ancient quarrel which had plagued relations between
Scotland and England ever since Edward I adjudicated 'the
Great Cause' between the various competitors to the Scottish
throne at Norham Castle in May 1291. The next day Henry
gave Lyon Herald a coldly threatening reply for James. Henry
wrote that he had suspected 'unsteadfastness' from James:

> We cannot marvel, considering the ancient accustomed
> manner of your progenitors, who never longer kept faith
> and promise than pleased them.

He continued that if James broke the peace and invaded
England:

> he shall have enough to do whensoever he beginneth: and
> also I trusted him not so well but I provided for him right
> well, and that shall he well know.[4]

This exchange of letters between James and Henry made
the breach between Scotland and England open and war

inevitable, but it had taken many years of hard negotiation and stormy council meetings to reach this point. The war of 1513 was not simply a periodic revival of the perennial quarrel between Scotland and England. James's support for the French king, Louis XII, embroiled Scotland in a much wider European struggle. In 1513, virtually the whole of Europe was at war. The conflict revolved around French ambitions in Italy, and by 1513 Louis XII of France found the 'Holy League' comprised of the pope, the Emperor-elect Maximilian and the young Henry VIII ranged against him. The 'Holy League' was a diverse coalition of competing interests which broke up rapidly in 1514. However in 1513, it was Henry VIII, the vigorous new king of England, who precipitated the crisis with Scotland.

Henry VIII was quite unlike his father. Henry Tudor, who became Henry VII, had been a bold adventurer as a young man and had gained the English crown on Bosworth field in 1485. Yet Henry VII never felt sufficiently secure on the throne to adopt aggressive or risky policies. Instead, Henry VII became intent on securing the throne he had won and promoted economy at home and peace in Europe. He had, to a large extent, jettisoned the continental ambitions of previous English kings and had avoided entangling his kingdom in the series of wars which flared up after Charles VIII of France invaded Italy in 1494.[5]

Henry VIII was born on 28 June 1491, the second son of Henry VII and Elizabeth of York, but the only son to reach full adulthood. As the second son, he was kept in relative obscurity at the royal palace of Eltham during his childhood, although he was allowed to 'rule' at Eltham and dominate his sisters, Margaret and Mary. However, in April 1502, his brother Arthur, Prince of Wales, died tragically at the age of fifteen. Henry then became Prince of Wales, and even eventually took Arthur's bride, Katherine of Aragon, after his accession. Yet, because Henry had not originally been destined for the throne, his father had not trained him in the arts and responsibilities of kingship.[6] When Henry VII died at Richmond Palace on 22 April 1509, his son inherited a throne which was stable and secure, along with perhaps the fullest treasury ever bequeathed to a new king of England. But Henry was not content to follow the steady path of peace and prosperity mapped out by his father. While his father had stocked the English treasury through careful management and avoidance of continental wars, and strengthened the hold of the Tudor dynasty over the English throne, such quiet policies were of no interest to Henry VIII. He had the brash confidence of a man who was born to power, and if his father had strengthened the position of the English king, it was now for him to use that power. Polydore Vergil noted that Henry was, 'not unmindful that it [was] his duty to seek fame by military skill'.[7] Henry VIII was eager to gain martial glory in a renewal of the Hundred Years War and he was determined that his military exploits would exceed those of his ancestors Edward III and Henry V.[8]

Henry began his reign with a public oath that he would soon attack the French king, but his advisors did not necessarily agree and his council signed a Treaty of Peace with France in March 1510. Many of Henry VIII's original council had been schooled in his father's policies and it took time for Henry to bend his council to his will. Developments in the international situation were also useful in Henry's pursuit of war with France.

The French invasion and occupation of northern Italy in 1494 had created considerable conflict and instability amongst the European monarchs and princes. Pope Julius II, who had once enthusiastically supported the French king as his main ally, eventually realised the threat posed by them to his own territories and became intent on driving the French from their conquests in Italy. In 1510, he launched his 'Holy League' against France. Initially composed of the papacy, King Ferdinand of Aragon and the Venetians, Julius was keen to secure further allies against the predominating military force of France in Italy. The French king responded to the new threat from Julius with a schismatic General Council of the Church in May 1511, which aimed to supplant or depose Julius as pope. However, this direct attack on the Church played into Julius's hands, who could now rouse the faithful leaders of Europe to his 'holy' cause. With Louis now a schismatic heretic, opposition to war with France within Henry's council was easily overcome, and Julius secured the willing Henry to his cause in November 1511 with the gift of the golden rose★, barrels of Italian wine and 100 Parmesan cheeses.[9]

Henry eagerly despatched military expeditions to begin his war against France, but while Henry's ambitions were unbounded, he quickly became frustrated by the dismal failures of English arms overseas. In 1511, even before he joined the 'Holy League', Henry had sent two small forces to the Continent. A force of English archers assisted the Emperor Maximilian against the Duke of Guelders in the Low Countries in an attempt to win Maximilian's favour. This

★ A symbol of papal favour.

minor military expedition had significant political consequences, as it was one factor which helped to persuade
Maximilian to relinquish his alliance with France and join
the 'Holy League' in 1513. In May 1511, another force was
despatched to assist Ferdinand of Aragon, Henry's father-in-
law, in a campaign against the Moors of Barbary. While this
might have been seen by Henry as a crusade of sorts, it was
not attended with success. Once the force (under the command of Thomas, Lord Darcy) reached Cadiz, Ferdinand
blithely informed him that he had decided to retain his
forces in Spain to defend his territory against the French.
Darcy was furious, but had little choice except to head for
home empty-handed. Even though the expedition only
stayed in Spain for sixteen days, the soldiers still managed to
run wild, killing several Spaniards in a drunken brawl under
the influence of the 'hot wines' of Andalusia.[10]

Undaunted by this failure, Henry agreed in November
1511 on a joint campaign with Ferdinand to attack Aquitaine
and thus to regain a major former English possession in
France. Thomas Grey, Marquis of Dorset, with a force of
6,000 men, landed at San Sebastian in northern Spain only
to find that once again Ferdinand had changed his mind. In
fact, Ferdinand had simply used the English force to mask
his intention to seize the kingdom of Navarre. Dorset and
his men languished at Funterrabia, while Ferdinand conquered Navarre. With his troops in open mutiny over pay
and suffering from disease, illness and hunger, Grey was also
forced to return home.[11]

The war at sea against the French fared even worse. A
tough battle was fought with the French off Brest on
10 August 1512 which ended in stalemate, but also in the

King Ferdinand of Aragon (Henry VIII's father-in-law and
inconstant ally) in council.

loss of the *Regent*, one of Henry's largest warships. Then, in
April 1513, the Lord Admiral, Sir Edward Howard, was killed
in a fierce fight with Gaston Pregent de Bidoux, the famous
French admiral. Howard had boarded Bidoux's galley but
had somehow become separated from his men and ship. He
was tossed ignominiously from the galley to his death.

Howard's title of Lord Admiral was then given to his brother, Thomas Howard. Henry VIII's military adventures on the Continent had certainly not begun auspiciously.[12]

However, these initial military adventures were not the real focus of Henry's attention. Henry was determined to lead his own military expedition to France and deal with the French king personally. Henry's desire to lead the expedition came from his burning need to achieve personal glory. As Niccolò Machiavelli, the Italian political commentator, wrote in *The Prince*:

> Nothing makes a prince more esteemed than great undertakings and examples of his unusual talents.[13]

Henry's invasion of France in 1513 was to be a 'great undertaking' which would make Henry's reputation as a great prince and a brave military leader worthy of respect in all the courts of Europe. While most of Henry's erstwhile allies were vaguely amused by such unrealistic ambitions, they certainly did nothing to discourage him. Indeed, Pope Julius II fanned the flames of Henry's ambitions. In a secret papal brief written on 20 March 1512, Julius promised to strip Louis XII of his title 'Most Christian King' and of his kingdom and confer both on Henry. The papal brief informed Henry that the pope would personally crown him king of France in Paris, but there was an important caveat. Henry had to defeat Louis and seize his kingdom before the papal promise could come into force. Henry would have to win the crown of France himself.[14] The English Parliament obediently revived the Plantagent claim to the French throne in their declaration of war against France. While

Henry's expedition would cost quite literally a fortune, and empty the coffers which had been so carefully filled by his father, such a major military expedition would demonstrate the strength and wealth of the new English king. Henry himself would suffer no discomfort or real risk of injury during his campaign, but his quest for martial glory in France wrecked relations between England and Scotland and eventually caused suffering and death for many of his subjects – as well as for thousands of Scots.[15] In leading a direct and very personal attack on France, Henry left no room for James IV of Scotland to continue his policy of neutrality.

Even though relations with England had been under strain for some time before 1513, and the French king had made repeated attempts to renew the Treaty of Alliance with Scotland, James IV had continued to follow a policy of considered neutrality. This allowed James to maintain the Treaty with England which brought relative stability to the borders, while also allowing him to benefit from collaboration with France. This position of neutrality was one which had benefited James since 1502, and he did not abandon it lightly. Indeed, James IV had sent his faithful diplomat Andrew Forman, the Bishop of Moray, on numerous diplomatic missions, in an attempt to resolve the differences between Louis XII and the Pope. James had correctly identified the pope as the linchpin of the 'Holy League' but, unfortunately, Forman could not resolve the irreconcilable differences between the two men. When these efforts failed, James took the advice of his General Council and, after lengthy negotiations, renewed the alliance with France in 1512. The final version of the Treaty reached James in November 1512, along with details of the considerable military assistance the French king would offer Scotland in the event of war. Even then, James did not immediately declare for France in the European war. He may even have hoped that the renewal of the Treaty might make Henry VIII think before he embarked on a full-scale invasion of France. While James and his council were well aware that the two treaties were fast becoming incompatible, James wanted to wait and see which treaty would be the most valuable to maintain. There was never any real doubt that the French Treaty would prove the more important for James. Louis XII had made many offers of support to James if he would enter the war on his side, but on 8 May 1513, he made his most serious offer to the Scottish king. If the Scots invaded England when Henry embarked for France, and sent the Scottish fleet to France to co-operate in a naval campaign, Louis promised to supply and equip the Scottish fleet while it lay in French waters and to pay James 50,000 francs.[16] These considerable sums would allow James to conduct his war at very little cost to Scotland, while also ensuring the gratitude of the French king. Meanwhile, it was clear that Henry VIII would not only do nothing to halt the deterioration of his relationship with the Scots, but actively set out to wreck the 'Treaty of Perpetual Peace' between Scotland and England.

While Henry's 1513 expedition to France brought about the war between Scotland and England which led to Flodden Field, the roots of conflict also lay deeper than the immediate crisis brought on by Henry's aggressive policies. In understanding the chain of events that led to Flodden, we must explore the political situation in which all Renaissance monarchs operated. Niccolò Machiavelli's political commentary *The Prince*, while often pilloried as an example of amoral political manipulation, does give a real insight into the world of European diplomacy as it existed in 1513. Both Henry VIII and James IV existed in a political world dominated by a realist perspective of diplomacy and statecraft where power was measured in military might, and where the personal reputation and standing of the monarch was firmly linked to the respect accorded to his realm by other European monarchs. Both men understood the perilous nature of their positions: any display of weakness could lead to another prince undermining their position, or worse, any one of a number of powerful nobles challenging their right to rule.

There is little doubt that James IV was an effective and powerful king of Scots. From his birth in 1473, James had been kept firmly in the political background by his father James III, but in 1488 James escaped from Stirling Castle and joined dissident lords and nobles in open rebellion against his father. After his defeat at the battle of Sauchieburn that same year, James III was mysteriously murdered. Proclaimed the new king of Scots, James was, however, always aware of his guilt in his father's death. While Henry VIII had lived a relatively sheltered life at Eltham, James had direct personal experience of what could happen to a king of Scots if he pursued mistaken or unpopular policies. His minority had been dominated by the powerful nobles who had rebelled against his father, yet James had succeeded in taking power personally in 1492 with little in the way of bloodshed. James proceeded to bring about a remarkable level of stability and unity to Scottish politics. He avoided the favouritism that had ruined his father, and managed to stabilise the Scots' currency.[17] In 1493 he finally broke the power of the Lord of the Isles, whose seaborne empire in the Highlands and islands of Scotland had once challenged the power of the Scottish kings.

While the Highlands and islands of Scotland remained unruly and, in reality, beyond the full control of the king of Scots, James had mounted a series of successful campaigns to 'daunt the Isles' during his reign.[18] James IV also had the distinction of being the last king of Scots who spoke 'the language of the savages who live in some parts of Scotland and on the islands',[19] as well as being one of the few kings who could command loyalty from some of the chiefs of the Highlands, most notably the Earls of Huntly, Lennox and Argyll.

James also had a deep personal piety, which manifested itself in his enthusiasm for pilgrimages to shrines across Scotland – penitential services in remembrance of his father – and the dream of leading a crusade against the Turks. However, the frequent references in his diplomatic correspondence to his desire to lead a crusade have often been misinterpreted. James IV's ideas of leading a crusade has generally been seen as proof that the Scottish king was a naïve dreamer. In fact, after the loss of Constantinople to the Turks in 1453, the idea of leading a crusade to the Holy Land had become fashionable again and most European monarchs, including Henry VII, discussed the idea at least in principle. There were also practical advantages to James's advocacy of the crusade. The concept of crusade enabled James to develop a range of diplomatic possibilities. Stronger links with the papacy could be developed at the same time as James sought financial and material support from the pope and the French king for his crusading adventure. Just as importantly, his plans for crusade gave James a useful avenue to tax the Scottish Church more heavily. James's crusading notions were derived as much from hard-headed realism as from religious piety.[20] In September 1512, Louis XII promised James that one year after peace had been secured in Europe, he would give James a tithe from all his lands and supply cavalry, infantry, cannon and munitions for a crusade. While these were extravagant promises, James certainly utilised them to gain the best possible price for his real war against England in 1513.[21]

James IV also oversaw the growth of a distinctively Scottish devotional nationalism. He cultivated the friendship of the papacy which resulted in the gift of the most prestigious of papal gifts, the papal Sword and Hat, in 1504★. James's skilful handling of the Scottish Church had resulted in a united Church which stood behind its secular ruler. William Elphinstone, the Bishop of Aberdeen and the founder of Aberdeen University, discovered seventy new Scottish saints to supplant the English orientated list which had been used previously. Friendly relations with the papacy also meant that James was generally able to nominate the successors to vacant livings and to ensure that the Scottish Church was loyal to him.[22] His pilgrimages to the shrines of St Duthac at Tain in Wester Ross, and to Whithorn Abbey in Dumfriesshire meant that he travelled his country like few other Scottish kings.[23] In a very real sense, Scotland was bound together in his person.

James IV also placed a great deal of emphasis on acquiring an impressive military establishment, because he clearly realised that:

> Royal and national prestige could be enhanced by technological advance in the manufacture of artillery and the construction of ships.[24]

★ These papal gifts are now better known as the 'Honours of Scotland'.

Since 1508 the Scots had been casting modern bronze cannon at Edinburgh and Stirling under the direction of Robert Borthwick, the king's 'master meltar', with the assistance of a number of French gunners led by Gerwez.[25] While some guns were made ready to take the field with the Scots army, most were deployed on board the royal ships of the new Scots navy.

This new fleet of purpose-built warships fulfilled a number of important roles. Previous English invasions, particularly that of 1482, had underlined Scotland's vulnerability to seaborne attack. The Scottish fleet could help to protect Scotland and her trade from the raids of English privateers, as well as overawe the Highlands and islands.[26] Significantly, the 'Treaty of Perpetual Peace' signed with England in 1502 specifically excluded operations at sea from the terms of the Treaty. In building a powerful fleet, James could pursue an independent and possibly aggressive policy afloat without necessarily jeopardising the peace with England on land.[27] Just as the possession of a powerful 'capital' ship such as an aircraft carrier lends diplomatic and military weight to a state today, so the construction of large warships undoubtedly increased Scotland's prestige. James IV's expenditure on his navy increased throughout his reign, although it reached a peak in 1511–1513 when an estimated £8,710 Scots was spent each year.[28] The nucleus of James IV's navy was provided by two ships; the *Margaret* and the *Michael*. The *Margaret*, launched in June 1506, was a fine vessel of 600–700 tons with an armament of four falcons and one cannon, and was probably very similar in appearance and dimensions to its later counterpart, the English *Mary Rose* of 1509.[29] However, the pride of the Scottish fleet was 'the greatest ship that ever

sailed in England or France' – the *Michael*, which was
launched on 12 October 1511. The *Michael* was a truly
impressive ship of perhaps 1,000 tonnage and length of 180
feet, with twelve bronze cannon on each side and three enormous 'basilisks' mounted on the bow and stern in French
fashion. The ship was crewed by 300 men and able to carry
perhaps 1,000 more soldiers. This large craft was reputed to
have cost at least £30,000 Scots. Fully provisioned and
crewed, the *Michael* cost the treasury £500 Scots a month at
a time when the royal annual income was in the region of
£30,000–40,000 Scots. Louis XII's promise to pay for vict-
ualling and wages of the Scottish fleet once it reached French
waters in the summer of 1513 was therefore a major undertaking and would relieve James of a major expense.[30] If only
for a brief time, the *Michael* was the largest warship in northern Europe which ensured that the ship – and its king – was
discussed in courts across Europe. With a small but powerful
fleet, James could also claim, with some justification, that he
had the military power to lead a crusade – a useful tool in
his diplomacy which, until 1513, stressed concord amongst
Christians. More importantly, the possession of two impressive but expensive capital warships, constructed with French
assistance, ensured that James IV increased his value as an ally
of the French king. When James finally went to war, the existence of the Scottish fleet ensured that Scotland achieved the
best possible price for her alliance with France.

Henry VII's careful fiscal policies allowed James to build
an international reputation as a patron of the arts, sciences
and military arts at a price that Scotland could (just) afford.
While the sums spent on the Scottish navy, artillery train,
royal buildings and patronage were small compared to the

amounts lavished on similar items by Henry VIII from 1509 onwards, the expenditure certainly strained the Scottish Exchequer. Nonetheless, the money was well spent. James could claim, with some justification, that he had a first-rate navy, artillery train, and a cultured, sophisticated court.

James had also indulged in the use of military force to improve his political position. In 1496, James invaded England in support of Perkin Warbeck, a pretender to the English throne. James was well aware that Henry VII had good reason to be paranoid about any challenge to his position on the English throne. James may or may not have believed in Warbeck's claim to the English throne, but he clearly realised that he could make political capital out of his support to the pretender. James may have hoped that such intervention in England might bring tangible gains, since Warbeck had promised to return Berwick and pay the Scots 50,000 marks for support. The invasion was also an attempt to stamp James's mark on the international stage, by ensuring that Henry VII treated him with the respect he felt he deserved.[31]

James invaded England on 19 September 1496, and plundered the valley of the Till in Northumberland for a few days. This invasion was little more than an incursion to annoy Henry VII as, in the following month, James went hawking in Perthshire, which was not the obvious action of a man bent on conquest.[32] In 1497, Perkin Warbeck was married off to Lady Catherine Gordon, the daughter of the Earl of Huntly, but with his political importance now exhausted, James was pleased to see Warbeck leave Scotland in July 1497. In August, James mounted a more serious attack on Norham Castle on his own account. The unprofitable siege lasted for a week and when the Earl of Surrey attempted to engage

James in a battle, James played with him – suggesting that ownership of Berwick should be decided either by a battle, or by personal combat between the two commanders. Surrey wisely declined the offer, and James slipped back across the border, leaving Surrey frustrated and forced to disband his army due to lack of supplies and bad weather. While both invasions had been abortive, James's army had done a good deal of damage to the local defences of Northumberland. At the same time, the campaign of August 1497 had provided an important exercise in the logistics necessary to move a modern siege train from Edinburgh to Norham.[33]

Henry VII had been assembling a full English army to deal with the Scots, but a rebellion which broke out in Cornwall in May 1497 in protest at the taxes levied for the Scottish war, diverted his attention and forces to the South West. Henry quickly agreed to a seven-year truce which was signed at Ayton on 30 September 1497. James had increased his status through these invasions, which demonstrated the utility of military power and proved that important advantages could be gained through the use of military force against England in the right circumstances. The Spanish ambassador to Scotland, Pedro de Ayala, reported that the Scottish king had seen 'the ears of the wolf' but not its jaws.[34] It is possible that James's abortive campaigns in 1496 and 1497 may have given him an inflated impression of Scotland's military prowess. The seeming ease with which Henry had signed peace after having been threatened, may have given James an unfortunate impression of the ease with which military power could be applied successfully against the English.

It was agreed that the Treaty of Ayton should become the much more impressive sounding 'Treaty of Perpetual Peace', which would be sealed by the marriage of James to Margaret Tudor, Henry VII's daughter. James's 'rough wooing' of England seems to have worked perfectly. The 'Treaty of Perpetual Peace', signed in 1502, was an important agreement between the two monarchs because it allowed for the resolution of differences through international courts which would examine each grievance. The marriage of the Thistle and the Rose took place on 8 August 1503 and finally cemented the 'Treaty of Perpetual Peace' with England.[35] The wedding was a lavish occasion designed to impress the English guests with the wealth of the Scottish king. While the extravagant celebrations did not impress the main English guests (who included the Earl of Surrey, James's erstwhile opponent), James had gained a useful claim to the English throne. After 1503, the vexed question of a possible Scottish successor to the English throne always exercised the minds of Tudor monarchs.[36]

The 'Treaty of Perpetual Peace' has often been hailed as the new beginning of harmonious relations, which were carelessly thrown aside by James IV in 1513. In fact, it is quite clear that the Treaty was framed by two monarchs who had taken the measure of one another and who both understood that peace would only last between Scotland and England for as long as it served both their interests. Since peace suited Henry VII very well, James was unlikely to break the peace either, as it also suited his interests of maintaining Scotland as a strong and stable state. Yet even once the Treaty was signed, the history of conflict and tension between the two countries did not evaporate overnight. Relations between Scotland and England remained under strain. James's ultimatum to Henry VIII in

1513 gives us clear knowledge of the main grievances which the Scots held against the English in 1513. These reveal the level of tension, and indeed violence, that existed between two countries which were nominally at peace with each other. Henry VIII had, in an act of petty spite, withheld her portion of their father's legacy from his sister Margaret, now queen of Scots. Margaret herself had protested bitterly in numerous letters to Henry, but had received no response.[37]

Perhaps the most deeply felt grievance held by James IV was the murder of Sir Robert Kerr, the Scottish warden of the Middle March. The border remained notoriously unruly and a constant source of tension between the two countries. When Sir Robert Kerr was murdered by John Heron, the bastard, Lilburn and Starhed, on a truce day, Heron and his accomplices had gone beyond the pale recognised even by Borderers. However, the Bastard Heron and Starhed had evaded capture and could not be brought to justice. Although William Heron, John Heron's half brother and the owner of Ford Castle in Northumberland, and Lilburn were given as hostages to the Scottish king, the issue remained unsettled.[38]

Naval conflict also gave the lie to the idea that the peace between Scotland and England was somehow perpetual. James IV relied on experienced, but independent, sea captains like Sir Andrew Wood; and the three Barton brothers, John, Robert and Andrew, for ships and naval skill, even once the royal ships had been built. In 1511, James issued them with letters of marque which authorised them to prey on Portuguese shipping. However, Andrew Barton interpreted his commission broadly and seemed unable to distinguish between Portuguese and English shipping. He was eventually brought to battle off the Downs by the English Lord Admiral Sir Edward Howard and his brother, Thomas Howard. Barton was killed during the battle, and his two ships taken as prizes. James insisted that Sir Edward Howard should be tried in the warden court for breach of the peace and the murder of Andrew Barton. Henry VIII's reply was inflammatory, although possibly accurate, in that he maintained that he should not be accused of breaking the peace simply because justice had been done to a pirate.[39]

However, it is easy to determine that none of these grievances, either collectively or individually, were sufficient to cause war between Scotland and England. It is quite clear that James had larger ambitions than simply to govern Scotland well. Having achieved stability and prosperity at home, James wanted to raise Scotland's prestige abroad. The discussion of James as leader of the Venetian force on crusade was ridiculous, but James was no doubt flattered that it was even considered. The flurry of activity by James IV in securing papal approval and gifts, building a small but prestigious navy, developing Scotland's ability to build high technology weapons, and declaring his willingness to go on crusade, all meant that Scotland and her king were being talked about in courts all across Europe. In a very real sense, these activities put Scotland on the map, at a time when even papal letters described Scotland as existing 'at the very ends of the earth'.[40] James knew that building Scotland's prestige and reputation had a very real purpose. Ultimately, even the most extreme anglophile Scottish king, James III, recognised that only the English ever made war on Scotland. A Scottish king who was known and respected in the courts of Europe would have powerful leverage against rough handling by an English king.

However, such an interpretation also suggests that the war of 1513 was one of choice rather than necessity for the Scottish king. This has generally been the view taken of James's decision to go to war against Henry VIII. It is often argued that in choosing to go to war, James risked his life and kingdom for the foolhardy and ephemeral objective of increasing Scottish prestige. Pitscottie informs us that one of the main reasons for Scotland's involvement in the war during 1513 was the appeal of the French queen to James's sense of knightly chivalry and honour. The French queen sent James a turquoise ring with 'a love letter' pleading that he would raise an army and 'come three foot on English ground for her sake'.[41] James IV's decision to go to war has often been seen as romantic folly.

However, James did not take the decision to go to war lightly or found his policy on romantic gestures. He had resisted Louis XII's appeals for military assistance throughout 1510 and 1511, but by 1512 James was caught on the horns of a dilemma: Scotland's reputation and security could no longer be built or maintained through a policy of peace and neutrality. Although James had cultivated strong relations with France, and French support and expertise had assisted James's development of the Scottish fleet and military power, he had been careful not to renew the Auld Alliance with France throughout his reign. Peace with England and support from France had enabled James to develop his kingdom, but Henry VIII's dreams of conquest in France wrecked this careful balance. Machiavelli understood this situation when he wrote:

A prince is also respected when he is a true friend and a true enemy; that is, when he declares himself on the side of one prince against another without any reservation. Such a policy will always be more useful than that of neutrality; for if two powerful neighbours of yours come to blows, they will be of the type that, when one has emerged victorious, you will either have cause to fear the victor or you will not. In either of these two cases, it will always be more useful for you to declare yourself and to fight an open war; for in the first case, if you do not declare your intentions, you will always be the prey of the victor to the delight and satisfaction of the vanquished, and you will have no reason why anyone would come to your assistance.[42]

James did not declare himself on the side of Louis XII until it was impossible to reconcile the Scottish position between England and France. With so many enemies ranged against him, Louis XII eagerly courted potential allies. In French calculations, Scotland might counter-balance the English threat by forcing Henry to divert forces to defend his own kingdom.

In January 1512, Henry VIII made his ambitions public. The English Parliament claimed not only the throne of France for Henry and voted a large tax to finance the king's expedition, but also revived the well-worn claim of over-lordship over Scotland. The English Parliament stated that the king of Scots was, 'very homager and obediencer of right to your Highness' and justified such an insulting state-ment with the excuse that James IV was already preparing for war.[43] This was a clear threat to Scottish independence – and to the prestige that James had worked hard to build.

James wrote to the Danish king, expressing these fears that Henry had:

> lately determined in Parliament to advance his arms, not only against the Most Christian King and the realm of France, but also against us. He urges as his excuse that he cannot invade France in safety, if we be left to ourselves… nor is there any doubt but that, if France were conquered, Scotland would be attacked by those folks, who now, by the daily increase of injuries, heed not the breach of the peace, nor choose to make restitution.[44]

James was certainly hoping to gain support from Denmark, but the English threat to his position was clear. By July, James and his council had renewed the Treaty of Alliance with France.

Nonetheless, for all the French encouragement, James still did not seek to break with England. While James had prepared for war, he continued to actively seek peace. The election of a new pope, Leo X, in March 1513, following the death of Julius II, did not alter the policy of the Vatican. However, James did not send representatives to the French schismatic council at Pisa but continued to correspond with the pope, in the hopes of lifting the threat of excommunication which hung over any break with England.

Henry VIII attempted a form of diplomacy in late March and April 1513. He sent Nicholas West, Dean of Windsor, as an ambassador to Scotland in an attempt to learn something of James's plans and, if possible, to secure a written promise from James that he would 'keep the peace' – in other words, refrain from invading England while

Henry VIII invaded France. West spent an unhappy and unprofitable time in Scotland. He was not even able to spy successfully on the preparations of the Scottish fleet. West was kept waiting for audiences with James, and when he actually met with the king of Scots he found he could not wring a direct answer from him. While West was attempting to gain an extremely valuable undertaking from the king of Scots, he had nothing to offer apart from barely concealed threats of what would happen if Scotland broke the 'Treaty of Perpetual Peace'.[45] West re-emphasised the fact that if James broke the Treaty, he would immediately face excommunication by the pope. Even this did not dissuade James, who replied that:

> if he were disposed to make your Grace war he would not tarry for the Pope's monition; but he saith he will never make you war without he warn you by his herald, so that you shall have time to come and defend your own.[46]

Even then, James temporised and would not reveal his full hand, but merely stated that he would not break the peace unless Henry forced him to. West returned to England infuriated with James and with no clear answer. The delay and prevarication displayed by James may have been affected merely to ensure that West gained no valuable intelligence as to Scottish plans, but it also may have marked a genuine reluctance to make the breach with England certain.[47]

Early in April 1513, just three weeks before his ambassador signed the 'Holy League' in St Paul's, committing Spain to war with France, King Ferdinand completed an agreement for a one-year truce with France. Henry was furious that his slippery father-in-law had taken advantage of him yet again.[48] As late as 24 May 1513, when James heard of Ferdinand's truce, he wrote to Henry arguing that both Scotland and England had become parties to the truce and urged Henry to reconsider his attack on France. James offered to pardon all damage – the capture of merchant shipping, imprisonment of his subjects, and all such losses – and renew the peace if Henry would undertake to maintain 'universal peace in Christendom'.[49] This, of course, meant Henry abandoning his planned campaign against France. Not surprisingly, Henry scorned these proposals, but the correspondence does suggest that James was attempting to make a last ditch effort to construct a truce between England and France at least. Nonetheless, soon after this exchange of letters, James began his preparations for the forthcoming campaign in earnest.

The queen of France did indeed send James a turquoise ring in May 1513 and an appeal to advance 3 feet into England to save her honour. But this 'love letter' was accompanied with the final confirmation from Louis XII of the financial and material support he would give to James for the forthcoming campaign. Louis undertook to pay and supply the Scottish fleet while it served in French waters, but also to send substantial military assistance.[50] James did not manage to wring 2,000 veteran French troops from Louis XII as he had hoped, but the amount of French military help given in 1513 was considerable. James had held out for the highest bidder for his services in the great European war and he had received a handsome down payment from the king of France.

James wrote to King Hans of Denmark, in an effort to enlist his help against England, that:

> If aid be given to the Most Christian King, not only will all
> expenses be repaid, but in the future greater support will be
> given in return by the French King against our enemies.[51]

In many respects, these French promises formed the crux of the matter. By being a true friend to the king of France, James could hope to fight a successful military campaign and gain renown in his own right, while also gaining the gratitude of a powerful ally. In contrast to the substantial financial and military support offered by Louis XII, there was nothing but contemptuous silence from Henry VIII. West's embassy had merely reinforced the point. Henry would offer James nothing, not even a gesture such as finally sending Margaret her legacy, to preserve the peace. Instead, Henry had offered insults and thinly veiled threats to James. Under such circumstances, after having worked for over three years to preserve peace in an attempt to heal the breach between France and England, James had little option but to go to war.

The English threat to James IV and Scottish independence should not be underestimated. Henry was determined to go to war with France in 1513. This meant that James eventually had to make a hard choice; support England or France, because he could no longer do both. If James had remained neutral during the campaign of 1513, at some point his breach of faith, (if not of treaty) with the French king would have become clear. James would have abandoned his firmest supporter, who had given Scotland substantial financial and military aid. In the place of France, James could only look towards England and its new king who jealously claimed dominance over Scotland – and who would offer nothing to reward Scotland for her neutrality. Displays of weakness by

Scottish kings in the face of English threats had invariably brought disaster. Machiavelli warned that:

> a prince should avoid ever joining forces with one more powerful than himself against others unless necessity compels it… for you remain his prisoner if you win, and princes should avoid, as much as possible, being left at the mercy of others.[52]

In Machiavelli's opinion, there was no advantage in allying your state with a powerful neighbour who would gain leverage over your actions. Nonetheless, the meeting of the king's council in July 1513, to debate whether Scotland should support France in the coming war, was stormy. French ambassadors arrived at the Scottish court to ask for James's support against Henry's invasion of France. Opinion in the council was divided. William Elphinstone, the venerable and experienced Bishop of Aberdeen, who had been a loyal and wise member of the royal administration since the days of James III, argued against war with England.[53] Elphinstone reminded the king that there was, 'great need of deliberation in such a crisis', and feared the consequences if the English should turn their military preparations against the Scots. He argued that:

> Neither had the French such claims on the Scots, nor had the English done such injury, that they should take the field on behalf of the French against the English, a nation both wealthy and warlike.[54]

Elphinstone favoured sending ambassadors to Henry in a last ditch attempt to turn him from his declared course of invading France, and 'that they should wait the answer of

Henry'. However, the majority of the younger nobles believed that the time for diplomacy was over:

> Much abuse was thrown openly on Bishop William...
> because he had spoken, like a crazy old man, stupidly and
> imprudently, against the public interest, and against the
> inviolable Treaty and ancient promise.[55]

The Bishop of Aberdeen certainly did not deserve such abuse, but there was no further time for delay; Scotland had either to go to war against the English, or remain quiescent while her French ally fought the English alone. James IV's final decision to go to war with England had the backing not only of the majority of his council and the nobility of Scotland, but also of the people of Scotland. James IV's coming campaign would be a chance to punish the hated 'auld enemy' and 'nothing would be heard but forward'.[56] Had James IV broken with Louis XII and kept the 'Treaty of Perpetual Peace' with England in 1513, he would truly have become the prisoner of the next whim of Henry VIII. In many respects then, James IV had little choice but to break with England and declare war. In this sense, the war of 1513 was a war of necessity for Scotland, no matter how unwelcome it might have been. However, we should not see James IV as trapped in a web of intrigue spun by Louis XII, but rather as caught on the horns of a dilemma created by Henry VIII.

Nonetheless, we should not see James merely as a pawn played in a game between France and England. James understood both the risks and the great benefits which might be secured by war with England. His previous skirmishes with England in 1496-97 had brought stability on the border, long-lasting peace, an English wife and dowry and much greater respect for Scotland abroad. In a war which involved much of Europe, there might not be much room for neutrality, but there could be substantial gains to be made by Scotland during the conflict.

When James IV made his preparations for war, the main objective for the campaign was clear; James hoped to divert English attention away from France. If James and his army invaded England successfully, his stock would rise throughout Europe, but particularly in France. When the English reacted (as he knew they would) by sending an army north, James would meet it in battle. If he could defeat the English army, James would win unrivalled prestige for his feats of arms. James had achieved much throughout his reign, but he had never won a pitched battle – which remained the ultimate accolade for a Renaissance prince. Henry would be forced to halt his French campaign to deal with the Scots – and James knew from his own young experiences of the English invasion of 1482 that it was difficult to hold an army together in Scotland when the Scots simply evaded contact. Such an outcome would make Louis XII a grateful ally and might well chasten Henry VIII when he realised the mettle of his brother-in-law, north of the border.

Thus the Scottish invasion of England in 1513 was far from being an act of reckless folly which was doomed to failure. It was the considered act of an experienced and able monarch. There were considerable risks to the policy of war with England, but James knew that he had to accept those risks in order to reap the benefits of a successful campaign. At the same time, the risks involved were limited. While James can hardly have been expected to believe that Henry would leave his northern frontier unguarded or in the hands of 'millers and mass priests', as he is reputed to have said, James knew that Henry would take the bulk of English military might to France. James knew he could never hope to deal with the full power of the English army commanded in person by Henry, but a 'second division' force raised from the northern counties would be an altogether easier proposition. James was not proposing to march further into England than was necessary to force a reaction. Even in waiting for the English army to arrive, James retained the freedom of manoeuvre, because if conditions were unfavourable, he could still slip back across the border as he had done in 1497. It was only once the battle was joined that James would lose this flexibility. The battle would be the riskiest element of the entire campaign, but James was not frightened of taking that risk to achieve his aims.

In this way, we can understand that the chain of decisions which led to Flodden started with James's declaration of war. Each decision which James took during 1513 followed from the same logic. His decision to go to war, to undertake a campaign which would force an English reaction and to fight a pitched battle were all founded on the same assumptions; that a successful campaign would secure him and Scotland from English threats and add to Scottish prestige throughout Europe. In choosing this course, James was attempting to steer a course through the very treacherous waters of European diplomacy while also hoping 'to punch above his weight'. Rather than become trapped between the Scylla of English threats and the Charybidis of strict neutrality, he was attempting to follow an independent path for the strong Scotland he had built.

2

THE ARMIES OF 1513

The Scottish preparations for war in 1513 were unprecedented in their scale and scope. James IV took the field with the largest and best-equipped army that Scotland had ever sent to war. English preparations followed well tried methods which were thorough, and produced an equally effective fighting force. Yet to fully understand the armies that fought at Flodden we must also explore the nature of the revolution in military affairs which had taken place in Europe over the previous decades.

The art and science of war was undergoing rapid change during the early sixteenth century. In 1494, Charles VIII of France had demonstrated the power of modern artillery in his march through northern Italy,[1] while in 1503 the Spanish General Gonsalvo had proved the power of the new arquebus★ when his arquebusiers shot down the cavalry and Swiss infantry of the French army at the battle of Cerignola.[2] Military developments in infantry weapons and tactics, siege warfare and artillery were avidly studied across Europe, but it remained to be seen exactly which developments were true harbingers of the future.[3]

★ The arquebus was a new form of handgun.

However, although this was a great period of military experimentation, certain developments seem to stand out. First and foremost of these innovations were the modern bronze artillery pieces which had enabled Charles VIII to smash the castles and walls of the northern Italian city-states in a matter of months. Monarchs across Europe spent enormous sums ensuring that they too possessed the latest artillery pieces. Similarly, the Swiss armies of the late fifteenth century had earned a formidable reputation in battle. Armies equipped and trained in these methods seemed invincible, and repeated Swiss victories during the fifteenth century brought many converts to the Almayns manner, meaning German or Swiss methods. When Sir Thomas Howard, the Lord Admiral of England, noted in the *Articules of the Bataille*, written after Flodden, that the Scots, 'came down the hill and met with them in good order after the Almayns manner',[4] he had recognised, through his professional knowledge of war, that the Scots had been utilising Swiss methods at Flodden.

One of the converts to the Swiss method was undoubtedly James IV of Scotland. Advised and assisted by French military expertise, the Scottish army which marched to Flodden was as modern and capable a force as James IV could afford. While Scottish military tradition played a role in determining the nature of the Scottish force at Flodden, continental military developments and ideas were just as important. In order to grasp the strengths and weaknesses of the tactics and equipment of the Scottish army at Flodden, we must first examine the impact of Swiss methods on the conduct of war in sixteenth-century Europe.[5]

In 1513, Swiss infantry had an unrivalled military reputation across Europe. At the same time, there were important

Engraving of the battle of Fornovo, 1495, which saw the collapse of the Italian mercenary system against the modern French army. A pike column advances, supported by hand-gunners and artillery.

parallels with Scottish military tradition which made the adoption of Swiss methods by the Scots seem a logical extension to previous Scottish military practice. In common with Scotland, the Swiss cantons were poor and mountainous territories, which had also fought for their independence against an outside power which claimed feudal overlordship.

The Swiss had developed their reputation as the finest infantry soldiers in Europe through their fight for independence against the Habsburg dukes of Austria. In reaction to the Habsburg claims, the forest cantons had sealed the Eternal Alliance in 1291, which bound them together into the Swiss Confederation.[6] Through a series of revolts and battles, the cantons had finally earned their independence. The primary Swiss weapon at this time was the 8-foot-long halberd, a heavy pole-arm which combined an axehead with a point and hook for thrusting, pulling and hitting.[7] The victories of Swiss halberdiers over Austrian knights and men-at-arms at Morgarten in 1315, Laupen in 1339 and Sempach in 1386[8] had been just as shocking to the Austrian nobility as Stirling Bridge and Bannockburn had been to the English. However, when Swiss victories took them outside of their mountainous homeland, they found that the halberd-armed infantry were outmatched by horsemen in more open terrain. After the battle of Arbedo in 1422, when the Swiss had suffered heavy losses in a fight against mounted and dismounted Milanese men-at-arms, the cantons had taken the decision to make the pike their principal infantry weapon as a defence against cavalry and a superior weapon against steady infantry.[9] During the fifteenth century, Swiss armies came to be formed of pike columns augmented by contingents of halberdiers, crossbowmen and hand-gunners. Although the Swiss fought both the French and Italians, it was the series of campaigns fought against the Burgundian army of Charles the Bold that cemented their reputation as the finest foot soldiers in Europe.[10]

Charles the Bold, Duke of Burgundy, had the vision of building his disparate territories in Burgundy and the Low Countries into a solid block of land running from the Alps to the North Sea. With this accomplished, he aimed to challenge the power of the king of France and create a 'middle kingdom' between France and the Holy Roman Empire. Unfortunately, such aspirations included reviving ancient Burgundian claims to much of western Switzerland.[11] Charles's attempts to defeat the Swiss cantons ended in disaster. At Grandson and Morat in 1476, and finally at Nancy in 1477, the Swiss pikemen smashed Charles's army and put it to flight. Charles himself was killed by Swiss halberdiers in the rout after Nancy. With his death, Charles's lands were swallowed up by the French king and the Emperor Maximilian. Confrontation with the Swiss had brought utter defeat and tragedy to the Burgundian dynasty.[12]

This remarkable string of victories meant that Swiss equipment, formations and tactics were closely studied by the European powers. It was well known that the main Swiss infantry weapon was the 18-foot pike. This was constructed from a wooden stave, normally of ash, with a steel head roughly 10 inches long. The top end of the stave was often protected by 'langets', which were steel straps that extended down the shaft to prevent the head from being lopped off. At such a length, the pike was a cumbersome and heavy weapon which was virtually useless as an individual weapon. Another problem with the weapon was that, on the march, it had to be grasped near the head and trailed along the ground, because if the pike was held on the shoulder, the wooden stave tended to vibrate which made it very tiring to carry. The Swiss tended to transport their pikes in bundles on carts rather than have the men march with them. Swiss armies were not armed solely with the pike, although by the beginning of the sixteenth century, two-thirds of the soldiers were equipped with the pike.[13]

Grouped in the centre of the pike column, around the cantonal standards, the Swiss also deployed men who wielded the traditional halberd. If the momentum of the pikes was ever lost, the halberdiers would move to the front to engage in close combat with the enemy, thus opening up gaps that the pikemen could then exploit.[14] The Swiss also utilised hand-gunners and crossbowmen as skirmishers to screen and support the advance of their pike columns.[15]

Although a liability in individual combat, when used in a tight, unbroken formation, the pike was a formidable collective weapon. The deep columns of pike-armed Swiss infantry were in fact utilising exactly the same basic methods as the Greek and Macedonian pike phalanxes of centuries before. The Swiss formed up their pikemen shoulder to shoulder and in numerous ranks. When halted, the front rank kneeled with their pikes sloping up, while the second rank crouched with the butt of their pike held by their right foot. The third rank held their pikes at waist level and the fourth rank held their pikes above their heads, with the points sloping downwards. In an advance, the pike was held at chest height with the pike-head pointing down.[16] The men in the first few ranks of the pike columns were also well armoured. Most of them were equipped with a sallet, kettle helmet or burgonet to protect their head, as well as Milanese-style steel breastplates, which often had tassets attached to protect the thighs. These heavily armoured men ensured the momentum of the pike column. The fifth and succeeding ranks were less well armoured and held their pikes upright, ready to fill any gaps which might open up in the first four ranks. These formations presented an opponent with a bristling mass of impenetrable pike points. The pikes outreached any lance, spear, pole-arm or sword, which made it nearly impossible for any infantry to approach and attack the pikemen effectively. Similarly, horsemen simply could not penetrate the formation, as their horses would shy away at the wall of pike points, while the pikemen could stab at the vulnerable horses and riders. In defence, a pike phalanx could prevent any infantry or cavalry from attacking it effectively. In the attack, a pike phalanx could force cavalry to retire and simply roll over most infantry, enabling the Swiss halberdiers to slaughter any men who had fallen over or been wounded in the first rush. The rest of the opposing infantry would have little option but to flee from the steamroller that threatened them. The Swiss specialised in rapid attacks with their pike columns which opponents found very difficult to counter.[17]

Swiss tactics for handling their pike phalanxes were also well known. The Swiss divided their armies into three formations: the *vorhut*, or vanguard; the *gewaltschaufen*, or main body; and the *nachhut*, or rearguard. The *vorhut* generally contained the crossbowmen and hand-gunners, deployed between the ranks of pikemen or used as independent wings. The *vorhut* was used to skirmish and gain a foothold in the enemy position. The *gewaltschaufen* generally contained the bulk of the Swiss infantry armed with the pike, and with the cantonal standards and halberdiers in the centre. The *nachhut* either operated as an independent wing or sometimes as a link between the other two formations. The *nachhut* was generally smaller, and at the battle of Nancy was composed of just 600 hand-gunners.[18] Although Swiss tactics were actually very flexible and were adapted according to terrain and circumstance, it was generally accepted that their main

formation in battle was to advance their three main formations in an *echelon* formation. Machiavelli explained the Swiss
system:

> The Swiss regiments at present are also based upon the
> model of the ancient phalanxes and follow their method
> both in closing up their order of battle and in relieving their
> ranks; when they engage, they are placed on each other's
> flanks, not in a parallel line. They have no method of
> receiving the first rank, should it be thrown back into the
> second; in order to relieve each other, they place one
> regiment in the front and another a little behind on the
> right, so that if the first is hard pressed, the second may
> advance to its assistance; a third is placed behind both these
> and also on the right, at the distance of an harquebus shot.
> They have adopted this disposition so that if the other two
> should be driven back, the third can advance to relieve
> them, and all have sufficient room either to retreat or
> advance without falling foul of one another.[19]

While the *vorhut* advanced for some point in the enemy's
line, the *gewaltschaufen* advanced on a parallel course, but to
the rear of the *vorhut*. Similarly, the *nachhut* followed slightly
behind the *gewaltschaufen*. However, the *nachhut* could be
used as a reserve and would often halt before the decision
to commit the reserve was taken. With roughly 200 yards
('an harquebus shot') between each column, there was sufficient room for wounded men to retire and disorder to be
checked without any fear that the next formation would
collide with it. This *echelon* formation had a number of
advantages. It was very difficult for an enemy observing the

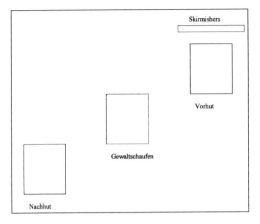

The Swiss *echelon* formation.

three columns to know where the main blow would fall. While the *vorhut* attracted the attention of the enemy and would almost inevitably draw the fire of the enemy, the other two columns were relatively protected and yet could reinforce the fight at any moment. Thus, the Swiss *echelon* method increased an opponent's uncertainty and confusion while providing distinct advantages and flexibility to the attack of the pike columns.

However, although the Swiss pike column possessed considerable advantages on the battlefield, the weapon depended entirely on cohesion for its effect. Any disorder in the pike column which opened up the ranks could provide a vulnerable gap which hostile horsemen or infantry could penetrate and exploit. In close, individual hand-to-hand fighting, the pike was a mere liability best discarded. Thus, rough terrain which made it difficult to keep formation could be very dangerous to a column of pikemen, and a very high standard of drill and training was essential to ensure that every man knew and held his position within the formation. Machiavelli called the Swiss the 'New Romans', not because of their weapons, but because of their Roman-like emphasis on training and discipline. While the Swiss forces were not standing armies, each canton placed great emphasis on the training necessary for war. Swiss soldiers were trained hard in the tactics and skills necessary to keep formation in a pike column. Every man was practised until the drills became instinctive, and this was essential in maintaining cohesion on the battlefield.[20] This emphasis on training also meant that Swiss pike columns could move with a rapidity and cohesion which other troops of the time could not match.

The collective nature of the pike phalanx also meant that the Swiss controlled their men with ferocious discipline. Swiss soldiers were renowned for their courage and bravery in battle but Balcus, the Milanese ambassador to the Swiss Confederation from 1500–04, reported that:

> When the Swiss start out to war, they swear a solemn oath that every man who sees one of his comrades desert, or act the coward in battle, will cut him down on the spot, for they believe that courage and persistency of warriors is greater when they, out of fear of death, do not fear death. They begin a battle after they have formed their phalanx according to the old methods of war, and steadfast and fearless, they are almost indifferent to life and death.[21]

Such savage discipline was necessary to bind the pike phalanx together and ensure that it maintained its solid front. Even one man flinching during combat could bring disaster. This ferociousness also applied to the Swiss treatment of their enemies. Having never adopted the feudal system, the Swiss had not developed the habit of ransoming wealthy noble prisoners. At the same time, an ordinary Swiss halberdier or pikeman who was captured by an Austrian knight could only expect summary execution. The Swiss were noted for not taking prisoners, and any men who fell into their hands would be killed. Even towns and cities captured by the Swiss could expect to be pillaged mercilessly and their inhabitants slaughtered. This bloody reputation often gave the Swiss the psychological edge on the battlefield. It was not surprising that the mere appearance of a Swiss pike column on a battlefield could inspire terror in its opponents.[22]

Machiavelli commented on the success of the Swiss:

And such is the general opinion of the excellence of these principles, from the many remarkable services they have done, that ever since the expedition of Charles VIII into Italy, all other nations in Europe have adopted the same weapons and manner of fighting.[23]

It is unsurprising that monarchs all across Europe became interested in Swiss techniques. Both the French king and the Holy Roman Emperor had come off worse in battles with the Swiss, and wanted to understand how they could counter the formidable power of the Swiss infantry. Many European monarchs were also keen to hire the Swiss for their expertise and proven battle-winning abilities, and Swiss contingents could be found in armies as diverse as France, Spain, the papacy, Milan and Venice.

The French king, Louis XI, had first noted Swiss abilities when they fought against him at the battle of St Jacques-en-

Basle in 1444. After their victories over Charles the Bold, Louis had taken 6,000 Swiss pikemen into his service in 1480 and retained them for the rest of his reign.[24] Even after his death, the services of some Swiss pikemen were retained, and when Charles VIII invaded Italy in 1494, he marched with 8,000 Swiss soldiers.[25] The French considered the Swiss to be the dominant force on any battlefield, which meant that the French were even prepared to put up with the quirky nature of Swiss mercenaries. If their pay went into arrears at any time and for any reason, Swiss soldiers would either go on strike or simply march back home. The French saying 'Point d'argent, point de Suisse' meant precisely that: no money, no Swiss soldiers. Montluc commented that:

> I have seen the perversity of these people cause us the loss of many a town, and wreck the King's campaigns. It is true that they are veritable soldiers, and form the backbone of an army, but you must never be short of money if you want them – and they will never take promises in lieu of cash.[26]

Although the French made attempts to arm and train bands of French infantry in Swiss techniques, they never found them as reliable as the Swiss themselves. It was said that French captains only looked out for stout, strong men rather than men with stout hearts. Montluc noted that he had to dismount to fight with his pikemen to keep their spirits up and forced his officers do likewise, in order to ensure that his pikemen would remain steady in the first clash of arms.[27]

The Holy Roman Emperor also realised the need for infantry to match the Swiss. Since Swiss hostility to the

Hapsburgs remained fierce, he could not hire Swiss mercenaries and instead took the step of raising his own infantry equipped and trained in Swiss methods.[28] The earliest reference to *landsknecht*, meaning pike-armed infantry, comes from 1486, and soon the empire had organised large units of troops which emulated Swiss methods. The *landsknechts* tended to favour defensive formations and relied more heavily on the new arquebus than the Swiss. The *landsknechts* also utilised veteran soldiers, known as *dopplensolders*, (literally double-pay soldiers, armed with a fearsome two-handed sword) who advanced in front of the pike column and whose task was to break up the order of the enemy, making gaps for the pikemen to exploit. In common with French methods, the officers of *landsknecht* units tended to be deployed amongst the front ranks of the formation to provide steadiness and leadership at the front. Although originally raised as imperial troops, bands of *landsknechts* soon became mercenaries who sold their services to the highest bidder. They were not quite so concerned about arrears as the Swiss and they had no compunction about fighting other *landsknechts*. The *landsknechts* also developed a fearsome reputation in battle, second only to the Swiss, who not unnaturally hated these impostors. Nonetheless, the principle of emulating or hiring the Swiss was well established by the beginning of the sixteenth century.[29]

In this era of military change, Scottish kings had good reason to be fascinated, even obsessed, with the emerging military equipment, tactics and technologies, since the Scottish military experience of war with England had long been disastrous. While much of Europe was concerned with finding an answer to the Swiss military system, the Scots still had to find an answer to England's formidable military power. For the past two centuries, every major Scottish invasion of English soil had met with disaster. In the British Isles, the English longbow had dominated almost every battle since Falkirk in 1298.

English kings had far greater military resources available to them than the Scots, and had been able to afford large, well-equipped forces which had conquered Wales and very nearly subjugated Scotland in the thirteenth century. While English feudal armies had well-balanced forces of mounted knights, spearmen, slingers, and bowmen, supplemented by mercenaries, the relative poverty of Scotland meant that its armies had rarely (if ever) been able to compete on equal terms.[30]

In comparison with their English opponents, Scottish knights had always been poorly mounted, armed and armoured and Scotland had been forced to rely on feudal-levied infantry and dismounted knights since the battle of the Standard in 1138. Scotland had never been able to afford a balanced force of knights and infantry. Similarly, even though numerous acts of Parliament were passed encouraging archery practice, Scotland had not devoted the time, effort and money to training and building a powerful force of archers. The only useful force of archers which Scotland could raise came from the hunters and woodsmen who lived in the forest of Ettrick, in the borders. Instead, Scottish armies were composed of masses of ordinary peasants, merchants and townsmen who were raised through the feudal system and whose ranks were stiffened by the better-armed and equipped Scottish nobility. The traditional Scottish infantry weapon, carried by the masses of feudal levies was the 12-foot-long spear. This weapon was short enough to be used as an individual weapon in hand-to-hand combat, but also long enough for it to be used collectively in formation. Scottish spearmen were invariably poorly armed and equipped, possessing a spear, and perhaps a helmet and shield, but little else.

Like the Swiss, the Scots had placed their faith in the collective use of their spearmen. The Scots developed their own formation, known as a *schiltron*, which was named after the round shield carried by the spearmen. The *schiltron* was essentially a round hedgehog of spearmen which the Scots used defensively against the English mounted knights. At the battle of Falkirk in 1298, Scots *schiltrons* had beaten off numerous attacks by English knights, but this battle had also demonstrated that such formations were horribly vulnerable to the Welsh longbow, which was used by an English army for the first time.[31] Bannockburn stood out as a notable success for the Scottish spearman over the chivalry of England. Robert the Bruce had taught his spearmen how to turn the *schiltron* into an offensive formation, and at Bannockburn, Bruce had utilised an *echelon* attack, similar to the Swiss method, to push an English army into a narrow neck of land and destroy it.[32]

But while Bruce and his commanders had scored other successes in battle such as Myton in 1319, his last testament advised future Scots commanders to avoid battle where possible and to maximise advantages in raiding and night attacks. This wise advice was often heeded in the coming years, but was not always useful for Scottish kings and their armies facing English forces. Just as the Scottish spearmen had developed techniques to defeat English knights, the English men-at-arms

Woodcut of a well-armoured
Dopplensolder Landsknecht.

began to fight dismounted, and English armies came to rely on the long-range killing power of the longbow.[33]

The large formations of Scots spearmen met with disaster against the English combination of archers and men-at-arms on every battlefield for the next 150 years. At Halidon Hill in 1333, Scottish spearmen, led by their nobles, had struggled through a marsh and then attempted to climb up a steep hill towards the waiting English army. Few Scots reached the English lines in the face of showers of arrows from the English longbowmen.[34] Neville's Cross in 1346 and Homildon Hill in 1402 simply repeated the disastrous experience which was shared by the French at Poitiers, Crécy and Agincourt. The English longbow remained the dominant weapon on British battlefields.[35] Thus, given the catalogue of defeats against the 'auld enemy', it is not surprising that the king of Scots would be receptive to any new military developments which might offer a better chance of neutralising English military power.

James IV was by no means the first Scottish king to be interested in the emerging military developments. Faced with the constraints of a primarily infantry force of hastily raised feudal levies, Scottish kings searched for an answer to English military effectiveness. James I had attempted to encourage the use of the longbow amongst his subjects, but without much success, and later monarchs attempted to find other solutions. During the fifteenth century, Scottish relations with the court of Burgundy were cordial and it is clear that the Scots paid close attention to the military innovations undertaken by the Burgundian forces. Mons Meg, the famous bombard still on display at Edinburgh Castle, was a gift from Phillip, Duke of Burgundy, to James II in 1457. The gun had been cast by Jehan Cambier of Mons in 1449.[36] The transfer and exchange of military expertise is unlikely to have ended with this gift. Charles the Bold's military ordinances of 1471, 1472 and 1473 laid down a detailed organisation for a modern professional army of paid soldiers.[37] While there was little chance that the Scots could afford to adopt many of the finer points concerning pay, leave and uniforms, the Scots do seem to have fixed upon the Flemish 18-foot pike as a new and improved infantry weapon for their feudal levies. Flemish armies composed of pikemen had scored notable successes against French knights, most notably at Courtrai in 1302, and Charles the Bold utilised Flemish pikemen extensively in his armies.[38]

In 1471, the same year as Charles the Bold's Abbeville ordinance, the Scottish Parliament forbade merchants to import or sell pikes less than 6 ells in length (18 feet 6 inches). In 1481, this was altered to 5½ ells (17 feet 6 inches).[39] While these acts were probably honoured more in the breach than the observance, it is clear that the Scots had recognised the pike as a potential replacement for their traditional spear. This view was no doubt reinforced when Charles the Bold himself came to grief fighting against Swiss pikemen.

With the eclipse of Burgundy, the Scots could now only look to France as their main supplier of military expertise and equipment on the Continent. Since Swiss infantry formed the backbone of all French armies from 1480 onwards, the French undoubtedly encouraged the Scots to take up Swiss infantry methods. Indeed, it is just possible that the French may have seen similarities between the Swiss and the Scots as unsophisticated mountain peoples who had relied on infantry in their fight for independence against feudal overlords. Nonetheless, although the Scots Parliament had passed the legislation in 1471 ordering the transition away from the spear in favour of the pike, it is also clear that few concrete measures were actually taken before the war of 1513. Re-equipping the entire Scottish army with a new infantry weapon was an extremely expensive task, and one which took a back seat to the other expensive military concerns of the Scots navy and artillery. Instead, the re-equipment and re-training of the Scots infantry had to wait until war was actually on the horizon. In early 1513, English agents were aware:

that at Camphere in Zeeland the Scots daily shipped long spears called colleine clowistes, armour and artillery.[40]

Many of the pikes used by the Scots at Flodden came from the Low Countries, just as the original inspiration for the use of the pike had probably come from the defunct Burgundian court.

While James purchased many of the pikes himself, he also received a considerable potential boost to his military preparations when the French military mission landed at Dumbarton in late July or August 1513. A note in a Scottish nobleman's purse, which was found by the English after Flodden, gave considerable detail about the mission:

> To the western seaport of Dunbar [Dumbarton] the King of France sent to James IV King of Scots: First 25,000 gold crowns of full weight. Also forty cartloads of powder. Two pieces of great ordnance called cannons. Also a ship laden with 400 arquebuses and 600 hand culverins, with their shot. Also a ship laden with bombards and other engines, including 6,000 spears, 6,000 maces… and pikes. Also a knight, by name Dansi [D'Aussi], with fifty men-at-arms, and forty captains to command the soldiers.[41]

The importance of this French military assistance should not be overestimated. The mission arrived late in Scotland, which meant that the military stores never reached James IV's army during the campaign. It was only in late 1513 that the lords of council ordered the arms to be moved from Dumbarton to Stirling.[42] However, the French military mission brought not only considerable military equipment, but also up-to-date military expertise in the 'Almayn' method of war. Thus, while the French munitions remained in Scotland, D'Aussi and his men would have been conducted rapidly to join the Scottish host, probably just before it was fully mustered.

The forty French captains supplied to train the Scottish levies for the Flodden campaign would have worked hard to teach their raw recruits the basics of Swiss military drill in the short time available to them, and would have advised James on Swiss methods and tactics in battle. The Scots had long seen the pike as the most modern and effective weapon, and it is highly likely that they saw the pike, with its deep columns of men, as simply an evolution of traditional Scottish methods of spear and *schiltron*. Even the Swiss method of attack in *echelon* had been enshrined in Scottish military tradition as the tactic used by Robert the Bruce at Bannockburn. With his army re-equipped with modern weaponry, armour and trained by French captains who were experienced in continental warfare, James IV would have been confident that his Scots infantry would match the exploits of the Swiss.

Unfortunately, European interest in the pike as the cause of Swiss victories had concealed the many other factors which had led to Swiss success. The Swiss armies won victory after victory due to their training, experience, high morale and ferocious military discipline. Their tactical system also went much further than simply the use of the pike. Mounted crossbowmen, hand-gunners and, most importantly, halberdiers, were also all part of Swiss armies which enabled them to cope with many opponents. The Scots infantry that attempted to emulate the Swiss in 1513 were sketchily trained, had little real experience of battle and could not have the same confidence in their drills and tactics as the Swiss. This meant that the Scots adopted the same solution which the French and *landsknechts* had used of placing their captains, or noblemen in the front ranks. In fact, Scottish noblemen had considered the front ranks as their proper place in a formation since at least the battle of Bannockburn. Scottish armies were led from the front to give encouragement and steadiness to the more hesitant feudal levies.

Just as importantly, the Scots (apart from the Highland contingents) were all armed with the pike. The Highland contingents kept their traditional weapons of bow, axe and the fearsome two-handed sword or claymore, and relied for protection on little more than a saffron shirt. Only the chiefs and their wealthiest supporters would have worn any armour: possibly a helmet with a mail shirt or padded 'akheton' or jacket. The Lowland and Border troops were equipped with the pike, and were drilled in the latest continental techniques. There were no *dopplensolders* armed with two-handed swords within the pike formations and none of the crossbowmen, hand-gunners or halberdiers present in Swiss armies. This sole reliance on the pike made the Scots army much more brittle tactically, while at the same time the lack of experience and training meant that the Scottish pike columns would be much less adept and sure than the Swiss who they were attempting to emulate.

However, the Scottish response to English military superiority did not begin and end with the pike and Swiss tactics. Just as the tactics of armies had experienced great changes in the fifteenth century, so had the level of protection which could be given to men in battle. The armour worn by knights during the tenth to fourteenth centuries had been extremely time-consuming and costly to make. It was also easily penetrated by the arrows fired from cross-bows and longbows alike, and knights had required great helms and large 'heater' shields to give them added protection. As armourers began to develop real expertise in the production of plate armour during the fourteenth century, both the helm and the shield began to be discarded.[43] By the late fifteenth century, armourers could produce excellent quality suits of 'harnois blanc' (white harness, meaning full plate armour) which were fully articulated and protected every part of the wearer. Contrary to popular belief, this harness did not make the wearer a lumbering, immobile target, but instead was light and flexible enough to allow considerable freedom of movement. Just as importantly, the curved and fluted shape of the armour was specifically designed to deflect sword blows – and arrows. With a maximum draw force of 120 pounds, a longbow arrow had to strike plate armour at a 90-degree angle at close range to have any chance of penetration. By 1513, a man wearing a complete harness of plate armour had little to fear from a longbowman.[44]

While plate armour had been too expensive, when first produced, to equip the ordinary infantryman, by the early sixteenth century the techniques for its manufacture were well known and it was possible to produce relatively simple breastplates and helmets in quantity. James IV had established a 'harness mill' at Stirling in 1496 and had attracted French armourers to work there manufacturing armour. This harness mill is unlikely to have produced as fine armour as the best Gothic or Milanese armour, but the armourers did manufacture complete sets of 'white harness' for Scottish noblemen. Most of the Scots nobles could afford full or partial sets of the popular Milanese armour, which was less ornate, and therefore less expensive than the elaborate 'gothic' German armour favoured by Henry VIII. The harness mill probably produced quantities of basic 'munition' quality armour back and breastplates, sallets and tassets, to supplement the large amounts of munition armour procured by James IV from France and the Low Countries.[45] While most of the Scots army would still have worn jacks or brigandines (canvas jackets which had metal or horn plates sewn inside them, with perhaps an old kettle helmet and scarf for protection), the front ranks, composed of the Scottish nobles and their retainers, would have been heavily armoured and well equipped. Scottish endeavours in manufacturing armour of various types and qualities meant that the Scottish army at Flodden was certainly the best protected of any Scottish army up to that time.

Scottish kings were also fascinated by the potential offered by modern artillery. James II had developed an arsenal of guns and had been killed when a gun he was supervising blew up at the siege of Roxburgh Castle in 1460.[46] Gunpowder cannon were first developed in Europe during the 1320s, but it took much longer for them to become effective weapons of war. Early guns were constructed from either cast iron, or built up from bars and hoops of wrought iron. Such guns were enormously heavy and prone to metal fatigue.[47] After a number of firings, the metal fatigue could lead to bursting – with fatal results for the gunners. By the early fifteenth century, huge bombards were quite capable of smashing castle walls, but they were also so heavy that they were very difficult to move. Mons Meg was a very good example of the gun founder's art as it existed in the mid-fifteenth century. Mons Meg could fire an 18-inch-diameter stone ball to a range of 2,867 yards, which meant that the bombard was more than capable of knocking down a castle wall. However, the gun was also enormously heavy and difficult to transport. The bombard weighed 8½ tons and was 13½ feet long. Such was its size and weight, that Jehan Cambier had manufactured the barrel in two pieces which then screwed together to make transportation of the gun easier.[48]

In the late fifteenth century, however, gun founders began to cast guns from bronze. Bronze had long been used in the casting of elaborate, large church bells, and this expertise in fine casting was transferred to gun founding. Bronze guns were cast in one piece, thicker at the breech than the barrel, with a wood or clay former being used as an inner mould to create the barrel. The greater malleability of bronze reduced the dangers of metal fatigue, and a bronze gun that was about to burst generally gave some warning in the form of a swelling around the breech.[49] Bronze could be cast more accurately than iron, which meant that the windage (the gap between the ball and the barrel) in bronze guns was less, and the gun was thus more accurate when fired. Since they were stronger, bronze guns could take a larger charge safely, and fire iron rather than stone cannon balls. It was soon discovered that a smaller iron ball fired from a bronze cannon could inflict as much damage on a wall as a much larger stone ball fired from an iron gun.[50]

However, the scarcity of bronze made these guns very costly, and they became prized items in a prince's arsenal.

Imperator Cæsar Diuus Maximilianus
Pius Felix Augustus

1 Portrait medal of Louis XII of France.

2 The Holy Roman Emperor Maximillian, Henry VIII's ally in 1513.

3 King Henry VII of England, sketch by Jacques le Boucq in the Recueil d'Arras.

4 Sketch of James IV, by Jacques le Boucq in the Recueil d'Arras.

5, 6 The Great Seal of James IV (obverse and reverse).

7 King Henry VIII of England, whose aggressive foreign policy precipitated war with Scotland.

8 Modern memorial to Bishop William Elphinstone, an efficient servant of the Scottish crown for nearly forty years. King's College Aberdeen.

9 Portrait medal of Anne of Brittany, the French Queen who sent James IV a 'love letter'.

10 A model of the pride of James IV's fleet, the great ship *Michael*.

pictime varbeck natif de Tournay suppose pour Richard Duc d'Jorck second fils d'Edouard iv. roy d'angleterre l'an 1492. fut pendu à londres sur la fin de l'an 1499

11 Perkin Warbeck, the pretender to the English throne who was supported by James IV in 1496–97.

12 Sketch of Margaret Tudor, James IV's young wife, by Jacques le Boucq in the Recueil d'Arras.

Marguerite d'Angleterre Duigne espouse fille de Henry duc d'Angleterre femme de Jaques iiii roy d'escosse

13 Thomas Howard, 2nd Duke of Norfolk, who as the Earl of Surrey, commanded the English army at Flodden.

14 Stone panel of artillery at Edinburgh Castle, thought to date from the late sixteenth century. Mons Meg can be seen on the left, with culverin and equipment on the right.

15 Mons Meg, a fine example of the fifteenth-century gunfounder's art.

16 Norham Castle, the primary objective for James IV's 1513 campaign. The castle walls were destroyed by artillery in just six days, but were rebuilt and the castle remained an English border bastion until 1603.

17 Etal Castle, which fell without a fight to James IV's forces in September 1513. Lord Dacre brought the Scottish guns here after the battle.

Modern bronze guns demonstrated not only a prince's military power, but also his wealth and his patronage of modern technology. Modern bronze guns were thus one of the foremost symbols of a Renaissance monarch's power. Bronze guns were lighter than their iron counterparts, but French gunners also developed better carriages for their new bronze guns. The addition of trunnions to the barrel enabled the gun to be fixed to a carriage, but still elevated and depressed for firing, while carriages with large wheels and long trails could be attached easily to a team of draft animals. These features gave bronze guns much better mobility than the previous iron weapons.[51] Charles VIII's march through northern Italy in 1494 proved that a modern siege train could move with an army without unduly hampering its mobility – and destroy any fortifications which blocked its path.

James IV's interest in developing his artillery train thus had a deadly serious purpose. With a modern artillery train, James could transport his guns effectively to the border and then smash any of the obsolete English fortifications that he chose. A modern artillery train would revolutionise Scotland's ability to project military power where it mattered most. The artillery train taken by James IV to war in 1513 was one of the finest in Europe. There were five cannon, each one fired a 60-pound shot; two culverin, which fired an eighteen or 20-pound shot; four culverin pickmoyane, which fired a 6 or 7-pound shot; and six culverin moyane which fired a 4 or 5-pound shot, making an impressive total of seventeen guns in all.[52] Amongst these seventeen guns were Robert Borthwick's famed 'seven sisters'. It is unclear exactly which guns these were, but it is most likely

that the name was given to the five cannon and two culverin which had probably all been cast in Edinburgh Castle
by Borthwick. The movement of this large artillery train
required a major logistical effort. The cannon and culverin
were each drawn by thirty-six oxen and crewed by nine
drivers and twenty pioneers. The culverin pickmoyane were
pulled by sixteen oxen and served by four drivers and ten
pioneers, while the culverin moyane were pulled by a mere
nine oxen.[53] A mobile workshop complete with crane, tools
and an anvil followed the guns. The guns' 'stonis' (which
were probably solid iron shot)[54] were carried on twenty-
eight pack horses, along with twelve carts of gunpowder.
Robert Borthwick, the king's 'master meltar', or gun
founder, thus led twenty-six gunners, as many as 300 other
men, and 300 oxen.

While the Scottish artillery was up-to-date and crewed
by a paid, professional team of gunners, the bulk of the army
was raised on traditional, feudal methods. The king of Scots
had the right to call upon his subjects for military service of
up to forty days. A Scottish king could raise an army, but
its size depended on the willingness of his people to serve.
Although his nobles owed him feudal service, there was no
fixed obligation to bring a certain number of men. In an
effort to improve the readiness of Scottish armies, numerous
efforts had been made to enforce attendance at 'wappinschaws', which were held four times a year. Every able bod-
ied man was supposed to appear at these meetings, armed
and equipped according to his position in society. It is
unlikely that the 'wappinschaws' were universally observed,
and even less likely that such days included effective drilling
and training.[55] Not surprisingly perhaps, Scottish armies

relied on the nobles and their households to provide a stiff-ening element to the force.

While the king's summons of his people to war could be a dead letter if his noblemen simply did not respond to the call, James IV's summons in 1513 was amongst the most successful military call-ups of the feudal period in Scotland. The summons was sent to every part of Scotland including the Lowlands, Borders and the Highlands. Remarkably enough, noblemen, their retinues, burgesses and peasants all across Scotland responded to their king's call in 1513. This notable response gives a glimpse of the prestige of James IV, the stability and prosperity of Scotland at the time and the widespread popularity for the war against England.

It is impossible to give an accurate figure for the Scottish host of 1513. Many different figures have been given for the strength of the army. Hall mentions 200,000 but agrees with Holinshed in claiming that there were 'an hundred thousand good fighting men at the least' present at the battle,[56] while the *Articules of the Bataille* gives 80,000.[57] Pitscottie claims that James raised 100,000 men, but that through desertion was left with only 10,000 men apart from Borderers and countrymen. This figure is then revised to 20,000 men with the king and 10,000 Borderers on the day of battle.[58] The variety of figures given is symptomatic of medieval and Renaissance accounting concerning armies. Even today, the muster-strength of a military force can vary widely from day-to-day, and there were simply no mechanisms in place in 1513 to provide an accurate count of the troops in the Scottish force. It is impossible that James IV could actually have raised an army of 60,000 men let alone 100,000, and although it was common to exaggerate the size of an opponent's army, the high figures given by all of the contemporary accounts do at least suggest one thing: James IV's army at Flodden was one of the biggest forces ever raised by Scotland. In later campaigns, James V raised between 15,000 and 18,000 men for the invasion of England in November 1542,[59] while the Earl of Arran commanded a force of some 26,000 at the battle of Pinkie in September 1547.[60] These forces, however, did not contain as strong Highland contingents, nor were they raised with the broad popular support of 1513. It seems likely, then, that James's army in 1513 was roughly 30,000 strong at the battle of Flodden, and may well have mustered a maximum of 40,000 men at the start of the campaign.[61] A force of this size was certainly unprecedented in Scottish military history and would easily have lent itself to much wilder overestimations by the Scots, English spies and the soldiers at Flodden themselves.

With his careful development of the Scottish artillery train, and the modern equipment, training and armour of his soldiers, James had every reason to believe that he had found an effective counter to English military superiority. Well provisioned and supported by 'as goodly ordnances as any was in the world',[62] James had good reason to be proud of his army and confident in the forthcoming campaign when he marched his army across the Tweed at Coldstream, on 22 August 1513.

The English army which marched to meet James was a contrastingly outmoded force by the standards of the day. Tradition and conservatism had become a powerful influence in English military affairs. Henry VII had been unwilling to spend large sums on armaments, and had seen little

need to update English weaponry given the proven effectiveness of the English longbow and bill. In 1513, Henry VIII
sailed to France with an army of 24,000 men, comprising
the best of his men-at-arms, archers, billmen and artillery
train.[63] He had also hired large numbers of foreign mercenaries to provide an up-to-date cadre in his force, and Henry
hired 6,000 pike-armed *landsknechts* in France.[64] Meanwhile,
the Earl of Surrey, 'Treasurer and Marshal of England, Lord
Lieutenant and Captain-General of the said army'[65] was left
with the forces of the north of England which were raised,
armed and equipped in an entirely traditional way. The
English army which fought at Flodden looked decidedly
second-rate and behind the times.

English armies since the middle of the fourteenth century had relied upon a combination of dismounted men-at-
arms and longbowmen. By the time of the Wars of the
Roses, however, the men-at-arms were supported by soldiers carrying the English bill. The bill was an 8-foot-long
pole-arm, with a head not unlike the Swiss halberd.
Originally an agricultural tool for hedging and pruning, the
billhook had found its way into English medieval armies as
an improvised weapon carried by peasant levies. However,
the simple agricultural billhook was soon adapted into an
effective military weapon with the addition of a point on
the top and a hook on the back of the head. This meant that
the bill, with its spike, blade and hook, could be used to jab,
thrust and cut, while the hook could pull a man off his feet
or drag a knight off his horse. With the increased use of
plate armour by men-at-arms and ordinary soldiers alike,
the bill increased in numbers and importance within English
armies as it was perfectly adapted to smash, cut and punch

through plate armour.[66] The Venetian ambassador remarked in 1551 that English bills:

> have a short thick shaft with an iron like a peasant's hedging bill, but much thicker and heavier than what is used in the Venetian territories, with this they strike so heavily as to unhorse cavalry and it is made short because they like close quarters.[67]

Pole-arms outreached most swords and yet, given the weight of the weapon could also deliver a stunning blow to the head of an opponent. The bill, unlike the Scots pike, or spear, did not derive its killing power from collective use, but rather from the individual skill and strength of the man who wielded the weapon. Individual skill in wielding the heavy bill and in parrying the thrusts of an opponent was the key to successful use of the weapon. In combat, the billman, or the man-at-arms armed with a bill or pole-axe, held his pole-arm in both hands while keeping both his elbows close to the body. He kept his legs well apart for balance, and would fence, dodge and parry against the enemy's blows while attempting to land his own killing blow. The point of the bill could be used for a lucky strike straight through the visor of an opponent, or the hook used to rip the tendons behind the knee. The main aim was to knock, topple or hit the opposing man to the ground where the opponent, now lying desperately vulnerable on the ground, could be despatched with a quick thrust through the gaps in his armour.[68]

Although the longbow was originally a Welsh weapon, the English had recognised its qualities and began to use it in large numbers during the thirteenth century. By the fifteenth century it was unquestionably the dominant English weapon. Developing both the physical strength to pull a 6-foot 'war' bow and the skill to instinctively aim the arrow at a target took years of hard practice. When firing at long range, archers used lighter flight arrows which were unlikely to penetrate plate armour but would harass and wound more lightly equipped enemy soldiers. It was at closer range that the archer would use a much heavier pile or bodkin arrow with a square-pointed heavy head designed to punch through armour.[69] Yeoman archers were trained from boyhood in archery skills and this provided English kings with a ready-made force of skilled archers that no other European monarch could match.

The armour and equipment carried by the English archers and billmen at Flodden would vary enormously between the different contingents. The nobles, gentry and their household retinues would have been well-equipped with modern plate armour and good quality bills and bows, along with other personal weapons such as swords and pole-axes. However, the ordinary archer or billman might have been lucky to wear old or partial sets of armour and the vast majority of them would have worn ordinary clothes supplemented with a helmet and perhaps a padded jacket. However, many of the English soldiers would have ridden on a hack rather than walked on the march to the battle. English armies had long relied for their mobility on mounted archers who could travel much further and faster than ordinary infantry.[70]

The tactical system utilised by English armies was also well understood in 1513. In contrast to the deep formations composed of many ranks of men favoured by pike-armed infantry, English armies deployed in a linear, shallower formation. The men-at-arms and billmen would form up in compact lines roughly four or five deep while the archers, also four or five men deep, would deploy either on the flanks of the billmen in rough wedges or stand in front of the billmen. Thus, the archers were deployed to develop their maximum firepower at the beginning of a battle. However, as the two forces closed, the archers would retreat through the lines of billmen and take post in the rear when the two bodies came to 'hand strokes'. Once the English billmen were closely engaged with the enemy, the English archers would take up their secondary weapons of swords, knives or 'mells' (lead mallets) and join in the mêlée. This simple, yet effective tactical system had remained relatively unchanged since the battle of Agincourt in 1415. English armies had certainly had plenty of practice in using this tactic during the bloody engagements of the Wars of the Roses and subsequent military operations.[71]

The one element of the English army which was recognisably modern was the artillery train. The guns were commanded by Sir Nicholas Appleyard, whose normal function was 'Clerk of the Ordnance' but who acted as 'Master of the Ordnance' during the campaign while Sir Norton Sampson went with Henry VIII to France.[72] William Blackenall, also a 'Clerk of the Ordnance', served as 'Master Gunner' on the campaign.[73] While Scottish kings had placed great emphasis on developing their artillery trains since the 1460s, Henry VII had displayed little personal interest or enthusiasm for these costly weapons. However, Henry VII did still manage to accumulate large numbers of cannon and hand-guns during his reign, although many of them were obsolete types.[74] However, his son, Henry VIII, took an intense personal interest in the casting of new guns and soon increased English production of cannon dramatically. Even so, Henry was forced to turn to foreign gun founders for much of his requirement and, in 1510, an order was placed with Hans Poppenruyter of Malines for twenty-four curtows and twenty-four serpentines. These guns were delivered in 1512.[75] However, Henry VIII took all of his heavy guns with him to France for the sieges of Thérouanne and Touraine. This meant that Sir Nicholas Appleyard could only muster much lighter guns for the campaign in the north. Appleyard's artillery train was comprised of eighteen falcons, which were light field pieces firing a 2-pound shot, and five Serpentines which fired a 4 or 5-pound shot. These guns, crewed by 400 gunners and drivers, were mounted on light carriages for mobility.[76] While these guns were of no use for siege work, their mobility made them well suited for 'field' firing during a battle.

While James IV brought perhaps the largest Scottish army ever to war in 1513, the Earl of Surrey could only look to the northern burghs and counties for manpower. Northumberland, Cumberland, Westmorland, Durham, Lancashire, Yorkshire and Cheshire had all been excluded from the county musters which raised the forces for Henry VIII's army in France. While Henry had taken some northern horsemen with him to act as 'prickers' or scouts, he had left the military resources of the north more or less intact. In fact, Henry had kept a skeleton 'army against Scotland' in being from August to October 1512, under the command of the Earl of Surrey.[77] The English monarch never kept his border with Scotland entirely unguarded.

The English force was also raised by very different methods to the Scots army. The English government had relied on a modified form of feudal service to raise the large armies required to fight the French during the Hundred Years' War. Edward I had first established the system known as 'Contract of Indenture', which meant that, instead of relying on forty days' feudal service, contracts were drawn up between the king and his commanders which stipulated the number of troops required and the length of service. The crucial difference was that, under the 'Contract of Indenture' system, the troops were paid for their service. The king's treasurer would pay the commander a fixed sum for bringing a certain number of troops which the noble would then use to pay the troops under him. Each commander would bring his own retinue of household troops and supplement their numbers by sub-contracting to other nobles and gentry who also had their own retainers. The fact that the English soldiers were paid made a crucial difference. It meant that the army was a semi-professional force composed of reasonably trained, if not experienced, soldiers who would serve for as long as they were paid.[78]

While Henry VII had not sought to utilise his military machine unless necessary, he had certainly spent considerable time and effort ensuring that the system of raising English troops was overhauled and organised in a thoroughly efficient way. Henry VII had ensured that he knew exactly how many men could be raised from each county. 'Commissions of Array' were established to find out exactly how many archers, billmen and men-at-arms each earl, baron and knight could provide, which meant that Henry VII knew the total size of force he could raise and at what cost. Henry VIII inherited this efficient system from his father, and the Earl of Surrey relied on it to raise his force to fight the Scots.

The efficient Tudor mobilisation machinery means that estimates of the size of the English force can be much more accurate. The 'Treasurer of the King's Wars', Sir Phillip Tylney, had received large sums of money to finance the campaign and subsequently had to submit his accounts to detailed scrutiny by Sir Robert Southwell. The figures given in the English payroll give a very good indication of the strength of the English army. The tantalising problem with Tylney's accounts is that the accounts are based on the daily rates of pay and the amount of 'conduct money' to pay for the journey, 'from sundry places of the North parties unto the town of Newcastle' at the rate of eight pence for every twenty miles travelled. Thus, since each contingent made journeys of differing and unknown lengths, it is impossible to be certain of the exact strength. Nonetheless, reasonable estimates suggest that the English force was at least 20,000 strong and could have been up to 26,000 men strong.[79]

Another important piece of evidence comes from the fact that the Earl of Surrey provided the king with a document in 1514 which demonstrated that, by dismissing his army on 14 September, he had saved the wages of 18,689 men for a fortnight. While some men who were already dead might have been included in these calculations, it does give a reasonable guide as to the total strength of the force *after* the battle. The artillery gunners and his own retinue were not included in this total, which means that Surrey's total force after the battle amounted to 19,589 men. If the total number of casualties suffered by the English army at Flodden approximated 1,200 to 1,500 men, as is generally accepted, it would seem that Surrey's force was perhaps 20–22,000 men strong before the battle.[80] If, however, Surrey's army mustered 26,000 men before the battle as claimed by *The Trewe Encountre*, then the number of English casualties suffered during the battle must have been much higher than is generally accepted. These accounts also tell us other interesting things. The accounts claim that there:

> should have been to every c [100] aforesaid a great captain and petty captain there were in all the said number but xxvii [27] great captains and xii [12] petty captains.

Surrey claimed that this saved the wages of 149 'great captains' and 175 'petty captains', which suggests that either his force was badly under-officered, or his officers had suffered heavy casualties during the battle.[81] This brief reference in the accounts suggests that Surrey's army was not organised on the basis of a 100-man company, although this was the basic tactical unit in theory, if not in practice.[82] It would seem that the English contingents at Flodden relied on feudal loyalty and leadership, rather than paid captains and 'petty captains' who were unknown to them.

While the exact sizes of the various Scottish contingents and the exact loyalties and command structures which held them together are lost to us, we can gain some picture of the English force. Surrey collected his household troops long before the rest of the army was raised. These were captains, 'petty captains' and soldiers, drawn from his gentlemen and tenants which were used to form the core of the force. Surrey had a retinue of 500 men, composed of five captains, five 'petty captains', one 'spear' (this term denoted a fully armed and armoured man-at-arms who probably acted as Surrey's standard bearer), forty-three demi-lances (lightly armed and equipped horsemen who acted as scouts or 'prickers'), and 446 soldiers armed with bow and bill. There was also a headquarter's staff consisting of the Marshal of the Army, responsible for discipline, the Master of the Ordnance, the treasurer of the Wars, a pursuivant or herald, trumpeters, craftsmen and servants. These men all wore green and white 'coats' of the king's Tudor livery.[83]

We know that, in addition to these army troops, on 1 September, Surrey paid for twenty-seven great captains, twelve 'petty captains', fifty-five demi-lances and 11,406 other soldiers. These men came from many areas and regions but were all contracted to the Earl of Surrey himself. However, we also know that Sir William Bulmer was paid for his force of 200 mounted archers, which had kept watch on the border during August, while Ralph Brykenhed brought 1,988 soldiers from the lands of the Bishop of Ely in Cheshire and Lancashire. Surrey's son, Thomas Howard, the Lord Admiral, brought his retinue of 928 men from his ships. By far the largest separate contingent was mustered by Sir Edward Stanley. No fewer (and quite possibly more) than 6,500 men were drawn from the Stanley lands in the County Palatine of Lancashire and Cheshire.[84] The Stanleys had gained royal favour and gratitude after the battle of Bosworth in 1485, when Lord Stanley had kept his troops uncommitted until the vital moment and then attacked Richard III's men. Stanley's intervention won the day for the young Henry Tudor, who became Henry VII. The Stanleys were very powerful landowners who still held the balance of power in the north of England.

These were the armies which fought at Flodden. While the English army was very similar to the forces raised by their fathers and grandfathers in the Wars of the Roses, the Scots army reflected the great changes in military thought and technique which were beginning to sweep the Continent. Even so, both armies had much in common. Both were held together by feudal relationships but were riven by feudal rivalries. It is difficult at this distance in time to be conclusive about the motivation of the ordinary soldiers in these armies. Yet it is clear that the men of both armies marched to war beneath heraldic feudal banners which meant a great deal to them. Leigh of Baggerley, the Cheshire bard, tells us of the men from Cheshire and Lancashire who 'were wont at all wars to wait upon the Stanleys'.[85] Sir Edward Stanley and his brother, the Bishop of Ely, raised the men of Cheshire and Lancashire, who all wore the Bishop's badge on their coats. The Bishop's badge – an eagle's foot with the three crowns of the bishopric – was a modification of the Stanley crest of an eagle and child:

> *every man had on his breast, bordered with gold,*
> *a foot of the fairest foul that ever flew on wing,*
> *with three crowns full clear, all of pure gold.*
> *it was a seemly sight to see them together:*
> *Fourteen thousand eagle feet fettled in array.*[86]

Every man in the force wore a physical symbol of their loyalty to the Stanley family on their jackets.

Both armies which fought at Flodden were intimate reflections of their feudal societies. The individual soldiers served alongside men that they had lived and worked beside.

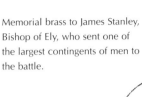
Memorial brass to James Stanley, Bishop of Ely, who sent one of the largest contingents of men to the battle.

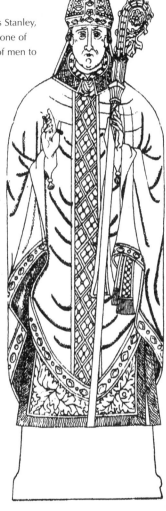

The eagle's claw, badge of the Stanley contingent, with the three gold crowns of the bishopric of Ely.

When the Provost of Edinburgh brought his contingent to the battle, the craftsmen, tradesmen and workers of Edinburgh were being led into battle by burgesses of the city that they knew, and sustained by the emotional and physical support of friends, neighbours and workmates.

Perhaps the closest modern example comes from the 'Pals' battalions of the First World War. The Earl of Derby received permission from Field Marshal Kitchener, the Secretary of State for War, to raise a battalion from the businessmen of Liverpool. Derby, a direct descendant of the Lord Stanley who had fought at Bosworth, utilised the principle, first developed by Sir Henry Rawlinson, that those who were recruited from the same area 'should be allowed to serve with their friends'. Derby's appeal for recruits was so successful that he became known as 'England's best recruiting sergeant'.[87] The 17th, 18th and 19th battalions of the King's Liverpool Regiment were known as 'Pals' battalions because they, like many similar units raised across northern England in 1914, were filled with men who knew one another. Derby had brought about the creation of fighting units which depended on a civil ethic and friendship for their morale and motivation. Derby's brother, F.C. Stanley, even took the 89th Brigade, composed of these 'Pals' battalions, to France in 1915. The soldiers of the three battalions had the distinction of wearing the Derby crest of an eagle and child as their cap badge, rather than the white horse of Hanover worn by the regular battalions of the King's Liverpool Regiment. Derby gave a silver cap badge to each recruit:

> It was a good badge, it was solid silver, you know, and we were very proud of it.[88]

Displaying a similar sense of pride to that which their ancestors felt wearing the same Stanley crest at Flodden.

The volunteer soldiers of Kitchener's army were proud of their local connections, and were sustained in combat by the relationships formed in their local communities. In exactly the same way, the vast majority of soldiers who fought at Flodden were not professional soldiers but civilians who were recruited by their local lord, bishop or burgess and who marched, lived and fought alongside men whom they knew. The men of Flodden were fighting for their king and their feudal lord, bishop or town, but they were also fighting for one another.

3

JAMES IV'S INVASION

Henry VIII landed at the English possession of Calais on 30 June 1513 amidst salvoes of gunfire celebrating his arrival, which could be heard in Dover. This represented the start of his campaign in earnest to seize the French crown. Yet instead of immediately embarking on a serious military campaign to wrest territory from the French, Henry kept the bulk of his men in Calais for nearly three weeks. The fore-ward and rear-ward of his army had already been sitting in front of the town of Thérouanne, in Artois, for almost a month when, on 21 July, Henry began to march his main body, known as the middle-ward, towards the town.[1] Thérouanne was a former imperial possession, and when Maximilian rode into Henry's camp with a small entourage, he offered to place himself under Henry's command. The Holy Roman Emperor-elect had omitted to bring the large army he had promised but was only too happy to call Henry, 'at one time his son, at another his King, and at another his brother',[2] while Henry did his fighting for him. While Henry's army was impressive and his household lavish, the siege of a small Flemish town was not another Agincourt.

While Henry attended to his campaign in France, he had left his queen, Katherine, as Regent of England in London and the experienced warrior, Thomas Howard, Earl of Surrey as his Lord Lieutenant of the North. On leaving for France, Henry turned to Surrey and said, 'My Lord, I trust not the Scots, therefore I pray you be not negligent'.[3] The seventy-year-old Earl of Surrey was the natural choice to command the forces raised by the northern counties in the likely event of war with Scotland. Surrey was an able and experienced soldier who had managed to survive remarkable changes in fortune. He had fought at Bosworth on Richard III's side, a misfortune which had led to his father's death on the battlefield and his imprisonment. The family's ducal title was forfeited. Somehow he had been able to convince Henry VII of his reliability, and had built a solid career as a faithful servant of the Tudor monarchy. Surrey also had more than a passing knowledge of James IV. He had led the English army to the relief of Norham Castle in 1497, when James IV besieged it and he had taken Princess Margaret to Scotland for her wedding to James in 1503. Even though he was the obvious choice to deal with the Scots, Surrey was furious that James had prevented him from accompanying his sovereign on a campaign in France. Surrey is reputed to have said of James, when ordered by Henry to organise the north:

> Sorry may I see him ere I die, that is the cause of my abiding behind, and if ever he and I meet, I shall do that in me lieth to make him as sorry if I can.[4]

There was a real sense of personal animosity between Surrey and the king of Scots once the campaign had begun.

Once Surrey had watched his king sail from Dover, he rode to London and began to organise his staff and personal retinue. These 500 'gentlemen and tenants' were mustered by Sir Thomas Lovel on 21 July and the next day Surrey marched north. Even before he moved north, Surrey had taken some matters in hand. Grain and supplies were being shipped to Newcastle, the muster point for the English army from 12 July.[5]

At Doncaster, Surrey ordered Sir William Bulmer to take a small force of 200 mounted archers and watch the border. By 1 August, Surrey had reached Pontefract where he established his headquarters and waited for news of the Scots. In this tense period of watching and waiting, Surrey was certainly not idle. Early in August, Surrey held a gathering of most of the northern gentry to choose commanders and set up a chain of command. The noblemen, knights, gentry, burgesses and bishops were asked to certify the number of 'able men horsed and harnessed' they could provide at an hours notice, so that the correct contracts of indenture could be drawn up in the event of a general muster. A chain of staging posts was established so that relays of messengers could carry orders throughout the north and thus mobilise the army as quickly as possible. Arrangements were also made to move the artillery train to Newcastle, 'so that all things, concerning that office were in a readiness'.[6]

During the summer months of 1513, while Henry VIII's army lumbered forwards on the Continent, much more serious preparations for war were being undertaken in Scotland. English agents on the Continent were well aware of the quantities of war stores that were being shipped to Scotland from the Low Countries in early 1513. Meanwhile, Robert Borthwick and the other gunners laboured to cast the final pieces of artillery to add to Scottish military strength. The

Scottish fleet was readied for service in June while stores of food were accumulated and extra taxes levied for the national effort. The mobilisation of sailors and soldiers for the fleet was not universally popular. Service in the fleet would require a much longer absence than the required feudal duty of forty days service, and would take the men far from Scotland. James IV sent summons across Scotland, 'for the furnishing of men to the ships', but the date by which the fleet was to be ready had to be revised from 1 July to 8 July, and finally to 19 July.[7]

James IV undertook a flurry of important activity in late July. On 24 July, James ordered the summoning of his feudal host to the burghmuir of Edinburgh. The proclamation was taken by messengers, 'through all the realm of Scotland', that all men between the ages of sixteen and sixty should be ready within twenty days with forty days' provisions.[8] Pitscottie gives a tale of 'a miracle seen' while the king was at Linlithgow Palace, praying for success in his expedition just after he had made the summons. A man 'clad in a blue gown' with shoulder-length yellow hair, appeared before the king and gave James the dire warning that, 'thou wilt not fair well in thy journey nor none that passes with thee'. The man also told James that he must not:

> meddle with no women nor use with their counsel, nor let
> them not touch thy body nor thou theirs, for and thou do
> it thou will be confounded and brought to shame.

After giving the king this dire warning, the man is said to have, 'vanished away as he had been a blink of the sun or a whip of the whirlwind'.[9] Much effort has been devoted to interpreting this tale of a prescient warning unheeded by the king. The man has variously been identified as an actor dressed as St Andrew or St James, and was probably sent by Queen Margaret to dissuade her husband from his preparations for war. However, the tale seems to give a dramatic portent of the king's supposed behaviour with the Lady Heron later in the campaign, and thus forms part of Pitscottie's explanation for the disaster at Flodden. It is most likely that this 'miracle', although a dramatic story, never actually took place.

Pitscottie also tells us that James raised his army hastily, and invaded England only because he realised that the French king would not receive support from the Scottish fleet in time. In fact, the mobilisation of the Scottish army was not done hastily; preparations had been going on for months. It was the day after James sent the summons to gather his army that the Scottish fleet, the greatest armada of ships that had ever been assembled by Scotland, sailed from Newhaven. The two great royal warships, the *Michael* and the *Margaret* were accompanied by private ships captained by Thomas Chalmers, William Brownhill and John Barton, along with some recently acquired ships which included the *Barque Mytoune*, a large former Spanish vessel, and the *Barque D'Abbeville*, a French ship. James IV sailed on the pride of his fleet, the *Michael*, up the Forth and bade farewell to his ships at the Isle of May.[10]

The next day, James sent Lyon Herald, king-at-arms, with his letter for Henry VIII, just as he had promised Nicholas West, so that Henry would know of his actions before he went to war. However, given the time it would take Lyon Herald to reach France, it was impossible that Henry would have time to come home to 'defend his own'. The next few weeks in Scotland must have been filled with activity as noblemen, gentry and burgesses gathered men, equipment and supplies for the coming campaign. It is unlikely that all of the troops assembled on the burghmuir of Edinburgh, but it probably was the muster point for most of the troops coming from further north in Scotland. The real muster point for the entire army was most probably Ellem kirk in Berwickshire, which had been the muster point for the Scottish army in 1496.[11]

The Borderers certainly did not muster at Edinburgh because, just a week after James's summons, Alexander, Lord Home, Chamberlain of Scotland, led his Borderers – perhaps as many as 7,000–8,000 men – on a raid of Northumberland. With many of the towers which protected the Till valley still ruined and in disrepair after the Scottish incursions of 1496–97, Home and his men were able to mount a very successful plundering expedition. Sir William Bulmer, who had been sent to the border by Surrey, could not prevent the raid, but mounted an ambush on 13 August when Home was returning to Scotland with his plunder. At Milfield, two miles north of Wooler, and within sight of Flodden Edge (where a few weeks later James would encamp the Scottish army), Bulmer's archers 'shot so wholly together' that they killed 500 or 600 Scots and captured 400 men, along with Home's standard and the plunder that the Scots had gathered. This inauspicious start to the Scots campaign became known as the 'ill raid'.[12] This unsuccessful raid was not accorded with the doom-laden significance of ill omen until after Flodden. Border raids between the Scots and English were common, and advantage passed between the forces quickly.

From an English point of view, the 'ill raid' was simply a sign of worse to come. Home's foray had given proof of what the English Border lords had long known; that Northumberland was open to Scottish depredations. While Hall's chronicle suggests that the raid was the 'first open token of war', it was still not clear to the English entrusted with the defence of the border what Scottish intentions really were. Thomas, Lord Dacre, seems to have acted as Spymaster General for Surrey. Hall informs us that Dacre was able to give intelligence to Surrey concerning 'the numbering and preparing of men in Scotland',[13] yet even after the 'ill raid', Dacre advised Surrey not to make obvious preparations or to raise the northern counties. Dacre was concerned that if the Scots realised that the English were preparing to fight, James would delay his mobilisation until Surrey was forced to disband his forces due to lack of supplies and the weather, which would then allow James to mount punishing raids into Northumberland with impunity. As a Border lord, Dacre was well aware of the danger of leaving the border exposed to Scottish raids, and as late as 17 August, he wrote to the Bishop of Durham suggesting that the impending Scottish invasion should be averted by buying James off.[14] It is possible that the payment of Margaret's portion of Henry VII's legacy earlier in the year might have been able to prevent war, but by 17 August, most of the Scottish host had mustered on the burghmuir of Edinburgh, ready to march south. War was now inevitable.

During this time, the king's artillery was hauled out of Edinburgh Castle, passed through the Netherbow Port, and started on the road towards the border. Pitscottie tells the story of a 'summons of Pluto' which occurred when 'they

Drawing of the lost memorial brass once at Lambeth of Thomas Howard, Earl of Surrey (later 2nd Duke of Norfolk), which shows the style of contemporary armour.

were taking forth the artillery' from the castle. A cry was heard at the Mercat Cross of Edinburgh, which was a 'summons of Pluto' (or the devil) demanding all men, 'both earl, lord, baron and gentlemen and all honest burgesses within the town' to appear before Pluto within the space of forty days. Only one man heard the summons and 'made his protestation', while all the other men mentioned in the summons 'perished in the field with the King's grace'. Even Pitscottie admits that this summons might have been proclaimed by 'drunken men for their pastime', and although the story is certainly atmospheric, and reflects the keen sense of anticipation and tension that must have pervaded Edinburgh at the time, it is probably a later invention.[15]

Once dragged out of the capital, the Scottish guns had to be pulled slowly all the way to Coldstream, forty-eight miles away from Edinburgh. This impressive, but heavy and ponderous, siege train would have required considerable effort to reach the border, but this large movement of guns had been practised during James's campaign of 1497. The fact that by 21 August,[16] the entire army with the artillery had crossed the Lammermuirs and reached the muster point at Ellem kirk, indicates the efficiency with which this campaign had been organised. On 22 August, the army forded the Tweed at Coldstream and marched to Twizelhaugh. James IV's campaign had begun in earnest.[17]

It was somewhat ironic that just as Scottish preparations for war were reaching fruition, Henry VIII's army in France fought its only significant skirmish of the campaign. On 16 August, a small body of French cavalry, which was attempting to give support to the beleaguered garrison of Thérouanne, was surprised at the village of Guingattes by a combined force of English and Burgundian cavalry. The dismayed French quickly turned away and the allied cavalry gave chase in what became known as the 'Battle of the Spurs'. Much to his chagrin, Henry missed this action which was the sole engagement of his campaign. Three days later Thérouanne capitulated, and Henry duly handed over his prize to Maximilian, who promptly ordered his troops to raze the town to the ground. Henry then turned his army against another French town, Tournai.[18]

At Twizelhaugh on 24 August, James held his last Parliament. An Act was passed which stated that the heirs of any man who was killed or died while serving in the army would come into their inheritances exempt from the feudal payments of wardship, relief or marriage. This has often been seen as a gesture made by a king who knew he was going to his death, but in fact, such ordinances were commonly made before battle in medieval Scotland. It simply meant that any noble man who fought in the king's army did not need to worry that the king would interfere with his estate if he died.[19] This was an important way of holding a feudal army together and may even have raised the morale of James's noble supporters.

Norham Castle, the Bishop of Durham's great border fortress, was the main objective for the Scottish army during the campaign. While Berwick-upon-Tweed had been the traditional target of Scottish sieges on the border (due to its importance and emotive value to the Scots), the capture of Norham, combined with the damage inflicted in 1496–97,[20] would unlock the English frontier and provide James with enviable strategic alternatives. James also knew that while Berwick-upon-Tweed was too tough a nut to crack, he could smash Norham's defences. His unsuccessful siege of 1497 must have provided his gunners with detailed knowledge of Norham's defences and their weaknesses. In 1513, with his modern artillery train, there would be no mistake.

Surrey ensured that the defences of Berwick were in order, and he also wrote to John Anislow, the Constable of Norham Castle, assuring Anislow that if he thought the castle was in any danger, he would march to Norham's relief, just as he had done in 1497. Anislow replied with confident bravado that he 'prayed God that the King of Scots would come with his puissance', because he would defend Norham for so long that King Henry himself would have time to return from France and raise the siege.[21] Anislow had every reason to be confident in his castle's defences, because Bishop Ruthal had been sending munitions and supplies to stock Norham since rumours of war began. Bounded by the steep banks of the Tweed to the north and west, and a ravine to the east, Norham's position was one of great natural strength. Bishop Flambard had first built a castle at Norham in 1121, and it had been progressively improved and rebuilt into a formidable English border bastion.[22] The outer-ward provided a first line of defence with a strong gatehouse to the west, while the inner-ward, protected by a deep moat, was dominated by the Great Tower.[23] Anislow's confidence would also have been buttressed by Norham's impressive record in repelling Scottish sieges. Although the castle had fallen in 1136, 1138 and 1322, the Scots had failed to capture the castle five times in 1215, 1318, 1319, 1327 and 1497.[24] James IV's recent failed attempts must have made Norham seem impregnable. At the very least, Anislow must have calculated that he could hold Norham until Surrey marched his army to his relief.

Local tradition suggests that James's artillery was initially positioned on the Ladykirk bank (the Scottish bank of the Tweed), but that a traitor from the garrison advised James to move his guns to the area east of the castle known as 'hang-man's land'. While it is unlikely that James needed the advice of a traitor to position his guns effectively, it is also clear that the eastern side of the castle was not an obvious place for bombardment. Protected from an assault by a ravine, the eastern side of the castle received much less damage than other parts which makes it unlikely that the Scottish guns were deployed against these parts of the walls. However, there may be some truth to the sequencing of these events. It is quite likely that James's gunners began the destruction of Norham even before the Scots army crossed the Tweed. Deployed on the Ladykirk bank, the heavy Scottish guns would have been able to fire destructive plunging shots directly into the castle. While Norham was a formidable medieval castle, it was not designed to withstand modern siege artillery and it was particularly vulnerable to artillery fire from across the Tweed. From the modern remains of Norham, and the evidence of its re-construction after 1513, it is clear that the riverside walls were comprehensively smashed.[25]

Once the Scots army had crossed the Tweed, the guns were redeployed to the west of the castle to batter the gatehouse. When James's artillery had been dragged into position, and his gunners had surveyed the range and elevation, each shot fired, at a slow but steady rate, would have hammered the walls of Norham into dust. Even so, James was unwilling to wait until the walls had been completely destroyed. The main western gatehouse of Norham was smashed during the siege, which laid the castle open for an assault.[26] Hall states that 'three great assaults' were made 'three days together', which proved just how important the quick capture of Norham was to James IV. He also states that Anislow 'valiantly defended' the castle:

> but he spent vainly so much of his ordnance, bows and arrows and other munitions, that at the last he lacked and so was at the sixth day compelled to yield.

After five days of bombardment, and three assaults, the outer walls had been smashed, or 'sore abated', although the remains of the great keep (part of which had collapsed) and the inner bailey were still in the garrison's hands. Anislow, running low on ammunition and well aware of his fate if he tried to hold on for a few more days before the Scots completed their destruction of his castle, surrendered on 29 August.[27] The English blamed the loss of the castle on 'the indiscreet spending of the captain',[28] but even the fact that the garrison ran out of ammunition for their guns tells us something of the intensity of the siege, and the inability of a medieval castle to cope with the power of a modern siege artillery train. King James IV had achieved the main objective for his campaign only a week after he crossed into England. His investment in new bronze guns had paid off handsomely. For the Scottish soldiers, who were wholly dependent on plunder for their pay during the campaign, the capture of Norham was a double triumph. Anislow was sent as a prisoner to Falkland Palace in Fife and his castle was completely sacked; the walls, gates and ordnance were all destroyed and the lodgings, with their furniture, arras (tapestries), provisions and wine all plundered by the Scots.[29] Thomas Ruthal, the Bishop of Durham, wrote to Cardinal Wolsey saying that this loss caused him 'great sorrow and pensiveness' and that he would never recover from the grief.[30]

While James had achieved his main objective, he did not intend to retreat as he had done in 1497. With his failure to capture Norham, there had been nothing to fight *for* in 1497, but in 1513 James would wait for Surrey and his army. With the prize of Norham in his hands, James had every reason

airnewzealand.com

AIR NEW ZEALAND

Carrier

HONG KONG

Destination

ELLIOT MR JOHN

Name

ECONOMY

Class

NZ38   21DEC

Flight   Date

47A

Seat   Airpoints™

Please be advised that you must be on board international flight
10 minutes prior to departure to avoid missing your flight.   077

A STAR ALLIANCE MEMBER

AIR NEW ZEALAND

Please be advised that you must be on board international flights 10 minutes prior to departure to avoid missing your flight.

airnewzealand.com

AIR NEW ZEALAND

A STAR ALLIANCE MEMBER

to defend his gains. If James took his army back into Scotland and left a garrison isolated in the ruins of Norham, nothing would be achieved and the campaign would be meaningless. Surrey would retake Norham and might then be in a position to threaten the Scottish border. In waiting for the English army, James was preparing to accept battle, but with time on his side he could ensure that any battle would be fought on his terms.

James ensured that his army would be ready to meet Surrey because on the day that Norham fell, Treasurer Hepburn was sent back to Edinburgh to bring up more ammunition, oxen and gun-carriage wheels.[31] During the first few days of September, the Scottish army captured the final English defences in the Till valley. Wark, Ford and Etal Castles fell in quick succession. After the demonstration of the power of the Scottish artillery at Norham, the threat of bombardment seems to have been enough to compel the surrender of these smaller castles. Ford Castle was defended by the Lady Elizabeth Heron, who probably surrendered on 1 September. James made Ford his headquarters for a time, while his army reduced the local pele towers and plundered the surrounding villages.

Pitscottie famously blamed the disaster which befell James IV and his army on the 'stinking adultery and forni- cation' which, he claimed, James had committed with Lady Heron, who was 'a beautiful woman'. There is certainly no other corroborative evidence that James and his son engaged in 'whoredom and harlotry' with Lady Heron and her daughter, nor that, even if Pitscottie's tale is to be believed, this led to the disaster at Flodden.[32] In fact, there is no rea- son to suggest that there was any dalliance between James

Engraving of the battle of the Spurs or Guingattes, fought on 16 August 1513, which illustrates the heavy armour of the mounted men-at-arms, the dress of the English archers and the flamboyant costume of Henry's hired *landsknechts*.

and the chatelaine of Ford. It is clear, however, that Lady Heron attempted to save her castle from destruction and gain the release of her husband, William Heron, who was held hostage in Scotland in the place of the Bastard Heron who had killed Sir Robert Kerr. It would appear that Lady

Heron offered to secure the release of Lord Johnstone and Alexander Home, who had presumably been captured during the 'ill raid', if James agreed to release her husband and spare her castle.[33] These negotiations are probably the root of Pitscottie's accusations, that Lady Heron, 'this wicked woman', gave to the Earl of Surrey 'the whole secrets of the King of Scotland and his army'.[34] In reality, the negotiations failed and Ford Castle was burnt to the ground. It is also quite clear that, whatever espionage Lady Heron may have carried out, the Earl of Surrey remained unaware of the real Scottish preparations for battle.

While Pitscottie believed that James's inactivity at Ford had been disastrous, his account gives us an entirely false picture of the Scottish army in the first few days of September 1513. James may have remained at Ford until 5 September, when his men burnt the castle, but he knew that time was on his side. Each day that passed favoured the Scots because, while some Scots soldiers deserted, the campaigning season was drawing to a close. James knew that the Earl of Surrey would be pounding his way north, gathering his men and marching them hard to reach the border as quickly as possible. Due to the bad weather conditions:

there had not been one fair day, nor scarce one hour of fair weather all the time the Scots army had laid within England, but great cold, wind and rain.[35]

It was far better to keep the Scots army in shelter and mount raids for plunder in the surrounding villages. Most importantly, James and his commanders had found a perfect position on the nearby hill known as Flodden Edge, where

they could encamp and deploy the Scottish army ready to
meet the English. The fortified camp and emplacements for
the guns would take time to dig, and James would have
been quite unconcerned at the passage of time – when the
English army arrived, his army would be ready and waiting
for them.

There is no doubt that during this time some Scots soldiers deserted the army and went home. We know that on
5 September, the day that James left Ford, the Edinburgh
burgh council noted with anger the number of soldiers who
had deserted and returned to the city with plunder.[36]
However, the date of this outburst is significant. It suggests
that men from the army had returned to Edinburgh *before*
5 September. It is quite possible that many, if not all, of
these men had been lucky enough to secure plunder from
Norham and were returning home with their loot. The
unreliability of feudal hosts which depended on plunder for
pay was the very reason that the English relied on the contract of indentures system and mercenaries for troops.
Pitscottie tells us that the victuals and money of the various
contingents were dwindling and that each of the nobility
sent one or two men home to bring more supplies. These
facts do not suggest that the army was disintegrating, or that
the Scots soldiers had lost faith in their king. Feudal armies
– of whatever nationality – were notoriously difficult to
maintain and keep in the field, and it was quite common for
men laden with plunder, or servants intent on securing supplies, to leave the army.[37]

While the total number of the Scots army did dwindle
over this period, the combination of plunder gained in the
Till valley and the fact that there were fewer mouths to

feed, meant that the rest of the force could stay in the field for longer. Out of an original force of perhaps 40,000 men, at least 30,000 remained under discipline and were ready to face the English challenge. Even with desertions, the Scottish army which encamped on Flodden Edge remained the largest and most formidable force Scotland had ever fielded.[38]

Throughout August, the Earl of Surrey had waited tensely at Pontefract for news of the Scots. Finally, on 25 August, news came to him of the Scottish invasion. He quickly sent messengers off in every direction to order the nobles, clergy and mayors of the seven northern counties to raise their men and march to Newcastle, which was the muster point for Surrey's army. Almost immediately, Surrey and his retinue began to move north, gathering troops as he did so. The earl was no longer the young, vigorous campaigner that he had once been, and his rheumatism sometimes forced him to travel in a coach. Nonetheless, the earl continued the march in the face of appalling weather. It was said that, 'his guide was almost drowned before him', but that the earl kept on 'to give example to them that should follow'.[39] Surrey was only too well aware that speed was of the essence if he was to reach the border in time. At York, Sir Phillip Tylney collected £10,800 from the abbott of St Mary's to fill Surrey's pay chest.[40]

Once Surrey reached the cathedral city of Durham, he stopped and spent a little time calling out the local contingents of the bishopric personally. After hearing mass in the cathedral, he asked the Prior if he could take the Banner of St Cuthbert with him to war.[41] This famous banner had first been carried at the battle of the Standard in 1138. Surrey was the commander of a Christian and Catholic army and he knew that such symbols could be important in stiffening the morale of his troops. While at Durham, the earl also learned of the fall of Norham. On the stormy night that Norham fell, it is said that Surrey feared that his son, Thomas Howard, the Lord Admiral, would 'perish that night upon the sea',[42] as he was still sailing with his men to augment his father's army. After a tiring journey, Surrey reached Newcastle on 30 August and found much of his army already billeted in the town. The next day, Surrey marched his army north towards Bolton in Glendale, just outside Alnwick, where he intended to 'take the field'.

Although the earl reached Bolton on 3 September, it was not until 4 September that the army was fully mustered there and Surrey was joined by his son, the Lord Admiral, with 928 soldiers and seamen from the fleet. His arrival:

> with valiant Captains and able soldiers and mariners… much rejoiced his father, for he was very wise, hardy and of great credence and experience.[43]

Surrey was glad that his son was safe and was pleased with these veterans who augmented his force considerably. At Bolton, Surrey organised his army into the units he planned to deploy in battle. Surrey formed his army into a vanguard commanded by his son, the Lord Admiral, and a rearguard commanded by the earl himself. Both the vanguard and rearguard were divided into a main body flanked by two wings. The English accounts also mention the lords, knights and captains who had been contracted to bring men to the army. Edmund Howard, Surrey's youngest son, lead the small right wing of the vanguard composed of perhaps 3,000 soldiers from Yorkshire, Lancashire and Cheshire, who were under the leadership of: Brian Tunstall, Ralph Brereton, John Lawrence, Richard Donne, John Bigod, Thomas Fitzwilliam, John Clares, Brian Stapleton, Robert Warcoppe, Richard Cholmondely, Sir Thomas Butler, Sir John Booth and Sir Richard Bold.[44] The Lord Admiral's unit comprised perhaps 6,000 men brought from Yorkshire and Northumberland by: Lord Lumley, Sir William Bulmer, Lord Scrope of Upsall, Lord Ogle, Sir Stephen Bull, Sir Henry Shirebourne, Sir William Sydney, Sir Edward Echyngham, Sir Thomas Metham, Sir William Gascgoine, Sir Christopher Ward, Sir John Everingham, Sir Walter Griffith, Sir John Gower and the Bishop of Durham's large contingent.[45] The left wing of the vanguard was commanded by Sir Marmaduke Constable, a veteran of English campaigns since the reign of Edward IV. He had another 3,000 men under the command of his family members: Sir William Percy, his son-in-law; William Constable his brother; and his sons; Robert, Marmaduke and William; along with soldiers brought by Sir John Constable of Holderness and other Yorkshire gentry.[46] Surrey's main body of the rearguard was smaller at 5,000 men, and was under the command of: Lord Scrope of Bolton, George Darcy, Sir John Rocliff, Sir Thomas Methine, Sir William Scargill, Sir John Normavell, Sir Ralph Ellicar, Sir Thomas Barkeby, Sir Christopher Pickering, Richard Tempest, Sir John Stanley with the Bishop of Ely's servants, Sir Brian Stapleton, Sir Richard Abdeburgh and the citizens of York.[47] Surrey's unit was flanked on the right by Lord Dacre's wing, composed mainly of Border horsemen from Northumberland, along with 1,500 men from the Bishop of Ely's lands.[48]

The left wing of the rearguard was commanded by Sir Edward Stanley and was made up of the 'residue of the power of the county Palatine and of Lancaster'.[49]

Surrey and his captains also discussed the strategic dilemma that faced them in a council of war. Surrey's main worry was that the Scots would retire as he advanced and slip back into Scotland without fighting a major battle just as James had done in 1497. Surrey knew that he did not have the supplies nor a sufficient logistic chain to invade Scotland. Indeed, the earl would probably have already been aware that his supplies would not last beyond 9 September. This meant that if the Scots did retire, Surrey would be forced to disband his army, which would allow the Scottish Borderers to return and raid Northumberland throughout the winter with relative impunity. These strategic pressures meant that Surrey had to seek battle with James IV. A battle offered Surrey the only opportunity to deal with the threat that the Scots army posed to the north of England. Surrey, of course, did not know that James IV was also eager to seek battle with him, albeit for very different reasons.

On 5 September, Surrey took the field at Bolton, raising the Royal Standard of a Red Dragon.[50] In an attempt to find and fix the Scots, Surrey sent an English herald, Rouge Croix, to James IV on 5 September. Heralds held a unique position within medieval armies. Heralds were used by commanders to deliver important communications to their rivals and could be used to negotiate the time and place of a forthcoming battle, as well as agree ransom sums and the name of a battle. In this sense, heralds acted somewhat like a modern United Nations peacekeeping observer. However, heralds also had an intelligence function. Although non-combatants, heralds were expected to gather as much intelligence as they could during their trips to an opposing camp. Surrey's letter to James has often been mistaken for an example of quaint chivalry, but its intention was deadly serious. Surrey wanted to be sure that the Scots would not slip away as they had done before, and also wanted as much intelligence about the Scots army, and its deployment as was possible.

Surrey's letter accused James of acting:

> contrary to his oath and league, and unnaturally against all reason and conscience had entered and invaded his brothers realm of England.

And furthermore once there, had done much hurt in 'spoiling, robbing and burning'.[51] Surrey also formally offered battle to James in the hope that the Scots would agree:

> He will be ready to try the rightfulness of the matter with the King in battle by Friday next at the farthest.

This formal letter offering battle appears strange, but it was intended to fix the Scots and also set a time limit to the challenge. Surrey knew that, after 9 September, he would have to disperse his army in search of food and shelter.

However, although such a formal letter was common-place in arranging a challenge between two armies, Thomas Howard, the Lord Admiral, also sent a letter which was highly unusual. In his letter, Thomas Howard taunted James and attempted to besmirch his honour. The Lord Admiral said that he had tried to fight the Scottish navy but it had 'fled into France, by the coast of Ireland' and he also reminded James that he was responsible for the death of Andrew Barton. Howard went on with the statement that:

> He nor none of his company should take no Scottish noble-man prisoner, nor any other, but they should die if they came into his danger, unless it were the King's own person, for he said he trusted to no other courtesy at the hands of the Scots.[52]

This was a blatant attempt to anger James, and thus ensure that, if the Scots did retreat without fighting, Howard could make it appear that James had been too fearful to risk an engagement. The offensive nature of the letter by his son makes it clear that the Earl of Surrey was desperate to bring on a battle and hoped that such an insulting letter would make the Scottish king more willing to defend his honour and prestige in battle.

Once these letters were delivered, Surrey expected Rouge Croix to give as full an account of the Scottish army's deployment and numbers as possible on his return. However, James was determined not to reveal any information about his army's deployment, so he detained Rouge Croix and sent his own herald, Islay Herald, to Surrey with his letter. This was also highly irregular, and Surrey kept Islay until an exchange could be arranged between the two heralds. Yet the earl was more concerned to read the Scottish king's reply. James agreed to wait for Surrey and his army until noon on Friday 9 September. Surrey was 'right joyous' at this answer, because it appeared that the Scots would stand to fight after all.[53]

On 6 September, confident that his prey would not now slip from his grasp, Surrey marched his army to Wooler Haugh, five miles from Bolton and only three miles from the position of the Scottish army. Surrey evidently imagined that the Scottish army would march from Ford and deploy for battle, on the:

> goodly and large cornfield called Milfield [scene of the ill-raid] which was a convenient and fair ground for two hosts to fight on.[54]

However, when Rouge Croix finally returned to Surrey's headquarters on 7 September, the earl received worrying intelligence from his herald.

The intelligence that Surrey received was so shocking that both contemporary English observers gave a clear account of the deployment of the Scottish army. *The Trewe Encountre* stated that:

> The King of Scots did lie with his army upon an high hill in the edge of Cheviot… and was enclosed in three parts, with three great mountains, so that there was no passage nor entry unto him but one way where was laid marvellous and great ordnance of guns… as goodly guns as have been seen in any realm.[55]

This description was echoed in Hall's chronicle which confirmed that:

> The King lay upon the side of a high mountain, called Flodden, on the edge of Cheviot, where was but one

narrow field for any man to ascend up the said hill to him, and at the foot of the hill lay all his ordnance. On the one side of his army was a great marsh, and compassed with the hills of Cheviot, so that he lay too strong to be approached of any side, except that the Englishmen would have temerariously run on his ordnance.[56]

These two accounts (although they are perhaps based on the same source) of the Scots' position on Flodden Edge are important. Since they describe a geographical feature which still exists, their basic accuracy can be checked. In fact, these accounts provide us with a surprisingly accurate and clear description of Flodden Edge. This suggests that, in basic details at least, we can trust these accounts. They also give us a sense of the immediacy and tone of Rouge Croix's original report to Surrey, and also highlight the seriousness of his position.

James may have exchanged formalities with Surrey and agreed to battle, but he had concealed his trump card. James had no intention of meeting the English army on a flat and level cornfield, where the English archers and billmen might well have the advantage. Instead, the Scottish army had dug itself into an extremely powerful defensive position on the crest of the hill known as Flodden Edge. The Flodden massif, an outlier of the Cheviots, was a mile-long saddle-backed hill, which rose to over 500 feet above sea level on its western and eastern sides. The Scottish army was encamped on its crest with their tents, huts, shelters and horses sprawling across its length. The right flank was protected by marshy ground while on the left flank the hill sloped very steeply down to the River Till. This meant that the Scots could only really be approached frontally from the south, which meant marching directly up the long steep slopes of the hill and the Scots artillery had been carefully dug in to cover this approach. There is also evidence that some of the Scots artillery were emplaced and sited to cover the River Till on the left flank of the position.

The use of an entrenched camp by a Scottish army was unprecedented and was almost certainly constructed on the advice of the French military advisors. Entrenched camps had become a feature of continental warfare in the first few decades of the sixteenth century. They were perceived as important additions to a defensive posture which could halt and break up an attacking formation. At battles such as Ravenna, entrenched camps had given real difficulties to the attacking force.[57] Rarely, however, did continental commanders have the good fortune to find as formidable a natural defensive position as Flodden Edge.

Even though the entrenched camp and artillery may have been modern innovations, James and his nobles *were* acting in the greatest Scottish traditions of Wallace and Bruce. The Scottish deployments at Stirling Bridge and Bannockburn had been carefully controlled to maximise the effect of favourable terrain. At Stirling Bridge, the English army had found itself surprised, and attacked when only half its force had crossed the Forth over Stirling Bridge. At Bannockburn, the English army had found itself compressed into a narrow area surrounded by Bannock and Pelstream burns which meant that they could not develop their full combat power. The nature of the terrain and the determined Scottish advance condemned Edward II's powerful army to defeat.[58]

With Flodden Edge, James had chosen a position which had all the advantages of terrain and which protected his army perfectly. If the English wished to bring the Scots to battle, they would have to hazard everything on a frontal assault against a prepared position. Once the English troops – tired by the climb, disordered and shaken by the Scottish artillery fire – reached the Scottish camp on the crest, they would be met by the formed Scottish pike columns, which would roll down the slope and wreck the English army. There is little doubt that, in adopting this defensive posture and plan, James was attempting to enhance the power of his force, while also masking its weaknesses. James, or at least his French advisors, was probably only too well aware of the sketchy nature of the Scottish troops' training and the brittleness of their morale. The advisors knew that manoeuvre on an open field required high levels of training and discipline, which the Scots soldiers simply did not possess. It would have been folly to expect them to fight on 'a convenient and fair ground', where the more experienced English soldiers and commanders would have the advantage. By entrenching his camp, digging in his guns and choosing a position with protected flanks, James was giving his soldiers every possible advantage to tip the scales in the Scots' favour during the coming battle.

It is also possible that James believed that he might not have to fight a battle. Secure in their formidable defensive position, the Scots could face down Surrey's army and wait until the English were forced to withdraw for lack of supplies. James had, after all, only agreed to wait for the Earl of Surrey until 9 September. If Surrey did not attack him before or on this date, he would be free to retire into Scotland, with his honour intact and leaving the Earl of Surrey just as frustrated as he had been in 1497.

But while the Scots' position on Flodden Edge must have given confidence to the men, and perhaps led to a certain amount of complacency amongst the Scottish commanders as good defensive positions have a tendency to do, there was one enormous flaw in the whole position and plan. Wallace and Bruce had both won astounding victories, but they had been astounding for the very fact that they had been totally unexpected by *both* sides. Both Wallace and Bruce had waited for the English commanders to make their own mistakes. At Stirling Bridge, Hugh Cressingham had made the foolish decision to march his army across a narrow bridge in the face of the enemy, mainly because he considered the Scots massed on Ailsa Craigs as a rabble incapable of fighting. Edward II had placed his army in a floodplain in an attempt to outflank the Scottish army and reach Stirling Castle, but had also calculated that the Scots would not act offensively. On both occasions, the English commanders had been trapped by their own mistakes which they only realised when it was too late.[59]

The problem was that James IV's position on Flodden Edge was too strong. It was obvious to the Earl of Surrey that his army would suffer heavily in a frontal assault on the position. With James's artillery practising ranging shots, and the Scots army almost visible from Wooler, Surrey was placed in a real dilemma. This painful fact forced Surrey to look for alternatives to mounting an attack which he knew would be doomed to failure. Surrey's desperation was revealed by yet another exchange of letters between the commanders. Surrey needed to draw the Scots out of their position, and he resorted to appealing to James's sense of chivalry.

On Thursday 8 September, the earl sent Rouge Croix, his herald, back to King James with a further letter requesting an answer by noon that day. Surrey asked whether King James 'would descend the hill to give battle or not' because, he wrote, the king's present position was 'no indifferent ground for two armies to fight'.[60]

James refused to see Rouge Croix himself and became very angry with the tone of Surrey's message. He sent his reply through a servant which was a calculated insult to both Rouge Croix and Surrey. The king replied that:

it beseemed not an earl, after that manner to handle a king, and that he would no sorcery nor had no trust of any ground.

He went on that he would:

take and keep his ground and field at his own pleasure and not at the assigning of the Earl of Surrey.[61]

James used chivalric forms, rituals and statements for his own purposes, but did not allow the concepts of chivalric honour or fairness to cloud his judgement. James may have been angry that a mere earl had the effrontery to address him in such a way and to accuse him of refusing to fight fairly, but it is also possible that his anger was feigned for the benefit of Rouge Croix. Surrey's attempt to use diplomacy and chivalry to even the odds failed. When Surrey received James's abrupt reply and realised that the Scots army would remain in its 'fortress invironde', he had little choice but to act.[62]

We cannot know whether Surrey's plan for the north-ward march was fully formed in his mind when he ordered his army to break camp and march for Doddington Moor. On 8 September, just after midday, on the receipt of

King James's reply, the English army struck camp (see Map 1). With the Scots entrenched in their formidable position, Surrey needed to do something to bring on a battle on more favourable terms. He decided to manoeuvre the Scots out of their position by marching around their flank. It is quite possible that Surrey was advised by the Bastard Heron, who had joined the English army, that it might be possible to attack the Scots army from the rear. Heron would certainly have known all of the routes, the crossing points over the Till, and the lie of the ground to the north of Flodden Edge. In an age before reliable or accurate maps, Heron's local knowledge would have been essential before undertaking the long flank march. Yet it is equally possible that Surrey began his march north without any clear idea of where he would go or what he would eventually do. He may have hoped to scout a possible route to attack the Scots in their position, or he may have hoped that, by placing his army closer to Scotland than the Scottish army, he might force the Scots to come down to fight.

Just north of Wooler, the English army crossed to the east bank of the Till, which gave them some protection on their risky flank march. As they marched north, skirting the high ground of Doddington Moor, they were only three miles from the Scots and often in sight of their enemy: 'and so forth over many hills and straits, marching toward the Scots on another side'.[63] That night, after a long march, the English army camped at Barmoor Wood, where they were protected by the 500-foot-high Watchlaw Hill from 'the danger of gun shot' from the entrenched Scottish guns. We can glimpse, perhaps, the scene through the poetry of *Scotish Feilde*, and gain some insight into the hardships of the common English soldier that night before the battle of Flodden. The poem tells us of the march and the scene as the last soldiers marched into the camp:

> *The rearward marched in array ever after*
> *as long as the light day lasted on the ground*
> *then the sun full soon shot under the clouds*
> *and it darkened full dimly and drew toward the night*
> *every man to his rest full readily him dressed*
> *beaten fires full fast, and fettled them to sleep*
> *besides Barmoor in a bank within a broad wood.*[64]

We also know that the soldiers, as they settled down wearily for the night, were hungry and thirsty. The stores and supplies of food hauled by the English army had been dwindling rapidly, and by the night of 8 September, there was nothing left for the soldiers to eat or drink. The men 'were hungry and much cold did suffer, water was a worthy drink, win it who might'.[65] The situation had to be desperate to force soldiers to drink water. Soldiers, and indeed the general population, would drink wine, ale or small beer, but rarely water. People understood that drinking water could lead to disease, and many military expeditions suffered terribly from dysentery due to soldiers having to drink water. These logistical problems illuminate the desperate nature of Surrey's advance. There had to be a battle the next day because the English soldiers' stomachs were already empty. This meant that Surrey could only hold his force together for a few more days at the most. After Friday 9 September, Surrey's army would start to disintegrate due to hunger, thirst, cold and dysentery.

Before dark, the Lord Admiral climbed Watchlaw where he 'perfectly saw and discovered them all'. Surrey was clearly anxious to learn if the Scots were reacting to his march, or if there was some way of attacking their position from the flank. As the admiral learnt, the Scots remained on Flodden Edge, but he could not discover an easy way to attack them from the flank. Surrey held a council of war that night and there were heated arguments concerning the next move of the army. Local guides must have told Surrey that there was another way to attack the Scots. Branxton Hill, which lay to the north and rear of the Scots' position on Flodden Edge, was not so steep which meant that it might be possible to march around the Scots and attack them from the rear. If the English could reach the crest of Branxton Hill before the Scots reacted, the English would find that the ground between Flodden Edge and Branxton Hill formed a shallow saddle which would be a 'plain field', suitable to deploy their forces. It was agreed (with some dissension) that the army would march north the next day, cross the Till at Twizzell Bridge and 'give battle to the Scots on the hill'.[66]

This manoeuvre to reach the Scottish rear was fraught with risk, and it is not surprising that some of the English commanders were doubtful of the plan. It was possible that the Scots might react by defending the crossing points over the Till, or that the English army might become badly strung out and open to defeat in detail. It would require efficient command and good march discipline for the march to be successful. By marching for the Scottish rear, Surrey was also deliberately placing his army in danger. With the Till on the left flank, and the Tweed behind them, the English army would have nowhere to retreat if they were defeated. A reverse on the battlefield would lead to rout and slaughter. It is a mark of Surrey's desperate position that he was prepared to take this risk, but it also reveals his confidence in his commanders. He knew that men like his son Thomas and Edward Stanley had the experience to keep the army together on the march and win the day.

Meanwhile, although conditions were probably more comfortable in the Scottish camp, the evening of 8 September was no less tense. Since the king and his nobles, as well as the French advisors, died on the battlefield the next day, our knowledge of the Scottish council of war relies on Pitscottie's account. There are almost certainly inaccuracies in his account as to the timing of the debates and quite possibly the content of the discussions. However, even allowing for Pitscottie's bias and heavy use of hindsight, we can approach something of the atmosphere which existed that night. There is little doubt that the king and his nobles engaged in heated debate, trying to divine what the English intentions might be. The Scots had seen the English marching north on the other side of the Till. This move was almost certainly unexpected and it left the Scots uncertain. Were the English marching to invade Scotland, or perhaps marching to Berwick where they could resupply? Was the English intention to attack the Scots from the rear? All of these questions must have fed the uncertainty surrounding the largest question in their minds; how should the Scots army react to the English manoeuvre?

Pitscottie tells us that King James returned from a reconnaissance to find his nobles in a meeting. Lord Patrick Lindsay of the Byres (Pitscottie's grandfather) was the main speaker at the council. Lindsay argued, and received general agreement, that they should fight the English as arranged and in the deployment which had been agreed upon, but that the king should not take part in the fighting. The king, he said, should be guarded in a safe place away from the battle.

In his arguments, Lindsay compared the Lords of Scotland and the Earl of Surrey to an honest merchant playing dice with a common gambler:

> So my lords, ye may understand by this you shall be called the merchant, and your King 'a rose nobill', and England a common hazarder that has nothing to jeopard but a bad halfpenny in comparison of our noble King and an auld crooked Earl lying in a chariot.[67]

King James was indeed precious to Scotland, and his loss in battle would be grievous. While the Scots might lose their 'rose nobill', the English were risking nothing more than a bad halfpenny and a rheumatic old earl. On coming into the tent, and hearing the discussion, James is said to have fallen into a rage. He vowed that 'I shall fight this day with England', and threatened to hang Lindsay by his own gate, swearing that though his Lords might all shame themselves by running away, they would never shame him by making him do the same.[68] There is little doubt that this story was definitely written with the benefit of hindsight, but it is possible that the Scottish nobles begged their king to remain safe during the battle. The Scots nobles were aware of the king's character and knew that he would want to fight in the thick of the action. Pedro de Ayala, the Spanish ambassador, had written of James's behaviour at the siege of Norham in 1497, that:

He is courageous even more than a king should be. He is not a good captain, because he begins to fight before he has given his orders.[69]

When de Ayala had questioned James on his rashness, the king had replied that:

his subjects serve him with their persons and goods, in just and unjust quarrels, exactly as he likes, and that therefore he does not think it right to begin any warlike undertaking without being himself the first in danger.[70]

Personal leadership had long been an expected attribute of a feudal monarch. At the battle of the Standard in 1138, King David had led his troops into battle.[71] On the first day of Bannockburn, Robert the Bruce had engaged in hand-to-hand combat with a young English knight, Humphrey de Bohun. When Bruce emerged victorious from the fight, his army's morale was raised considerably. In contrast, Edward II's flight from Bannockburn had brought on the final disastrous panic amongst his men. There were considerable risks to personal leadership on the battlefield. Richard III was killed at Bosworth, leading what he hoped would be a victorious charge, while David II had been taken prisoner at Neville's Cross in 1346.[72] Nonetheless, these were the expected risks and hazards of medieval kingship.

In fact, there is a striking parallel between King James IV and another famous Scottish military leader. John Graham, Viscount of Claverhouse (known as 'Bonnie Dundee'), led his Jacobite forces to victory at Killiecrankie in 1689, but met his death on the battlefield. On the morning of 27 July

1689, Sir Ewan Cameron of Lochiel begged Claverhouse to take no active part in the coming battle. Graham replied that he would consent to staying out of danger, but only after this first battle. He asked his commanders:

> Give me one shear-darg [harvest day] for the King [James VII and II], my master, that I may show the brave clans that I can hazard my life in that service as freely as the meanest of them.[73]

Claverhouse knew that only his person held together the competing clans which made up his small army. In just the same way, King James IV knew that his person held together his force gathered from all over Scotland. James was the only personal and symbolic link between his diverse lords, nobles, chieftains and burgesses. He led a feudal army that was held together by personal bonds of loyalty and service but was riven by personal rivalries and feuds between the Lowland lords. There were also the Highland contingents which did not understand the concept of feudal loyalty and had nothing in common with the Lowlanders or Borderers. King James IV was the living cement which held his army together. Just like Claverhouse centuries later, James had no option but to lead his men into battle.

There remained the uncertainty of what the English movements portended, and the Scots finally decided to wait until it was clear what the English intended to do. There have been many arguments extended over the years which have suggested that it was folly to remain inactive on Flodden Edge while the English marched around the Scots' flank. Pitscottie tells us that James said:

I am determined I will have them all before me on a plain
field and essay them what they can do all before me.[74]

Pitscottie claims that James spoke like 'a man that was bereft
of his wit'[74] but there was good reason to wait until the
English intentions became clear. James, or his advisors, knew
that the Scots army depended for its effect on artillery fire
and massed pike columns. If the Scots army left its powerful position without clear intelligence of the English intentions and manoeuvre, the army could well become
disordered on the approach march and might even be surprised by the English vanguard. A messy, confused encounter
battle would not enable the Scots to develop their full
combat power. It was, thus, a sensible military decision to
stay on Flodden Edge until the English intentions became
clear.

The English army broke camp at Barmoor Wood at dawn
on Friday 9 September. Soon after 5 a.m., the 12,000 men
of the vanguard and twenty-two guns marched off to the
northwest, followed by the 10,000 men of the rearguard.
The army left behind its tents and baggage and marched
only with its weapons. That day, the soldiers 'had no vitals
and were fasting'.[75] The troops marched north through
Duddo and then turned towards Twizzell Bridge and the
River Till.

The vanguard began marching over Twizzell Bridge at
11 a.m., although the whole crossing over the narrow stone
bridge probably took over an hour. There has been much
debate as to the exact ford used by Surrey and the rearguard to cross the Till. Every crossing point from Etal and
Ford to Twizzell Bridge has been suggested, but it would

seem logical that 'the Mylforde' mentioned by Hall is now known as Heaton Mill Ford. This ford is one mile south of Twizzell Bridge and would thus allow the vanguard and rearguard to remain within a reasonable distance. After his troops had crossed, Surrey made a speech to his captains, asking them to fight 'like Englishmen this day'.[76] Surrey's speech was certainly not the most inspirational, but it seems to have motivated his captains. His leaders responded that they 'would serve the King and him truly that day'.

Once over the Till, the English army, although strung out on the march, advanced in battle array towards Branxton Hill:

> then full boldly on the broad hills we pushed our standards
> and on a hill us beside there seen we our enemies were
> moving over the mountains: to match us they thought.[77]

The English army had to cross a marshy stream called the Pallinsburn before they could reach the village of Branxton, at the foot of Branxton Hill. The Pallinsburn stream itself, 'which is but a man's step over',[78] was not a serious obstacle, but the marshy ground which spread out on either side forced the English army to divide into two. The vanguard crossed the marsh by the Branx 'brig' which was a small causeway across the marsh and stream. This allowed the artillery to cross with the minimum disruption, while the rearguard swung to its left and crossed further east at Sandyford.

During the morning, patrols of Scottish Border horsemen must have shadowed the English force from a distance and given regular reports on its movement. Throughout the morning, it must have remained unclear to the Scots whether the English army was marching to Berwick or invading Scotland. However, between noon and 1 p.m., scouts would have ridden into the camp with the news that the English had crossed the Till and were marching south to attack the Scots army from the rear.

Hall's chronicle claims that Giles Musgrave, an Englishman who was the husband of one of Queen Margaret's ladies in waiting, warned James that Surrey intended to invade Scotland and raid the Merse. Hall remarks that Musgrave, 'did it for a policy to cause him to come down from the hill'.[79] However, this explanation for the Scots' move, which surely originated from Musgrave himself, is not convincing. After the battle, Musgrave would no doubt have been only too eager to gain some credit for the English victory, but when the English re-crossed the Till at Twizzell Bridge, the Scots commanders must have realised themselves that Surrey aimed to march on Flodden Edge from the rear.

We cannot know who made the final decision or under what circumstances, but James, his nobles and the French advisors were still making sound military judgements. If the Scots army remained in position on Flodden Edge, the English would be able to climb Branxton Hill and attack the Scots' position from the rear. The Scots army would have no great advantage of ground and would have the added psychological problem of being attacked from what had been their rear. Given the level of training and experience in the Scots army, this might well have led to confusion and panic. At some point, James decided to turn his army about and march it to the crest of Branxton Hill. This decision, and the ensuing march, was clearly taken in good time, because the Scots had time to deploy on the slopes of Branxton Hill even before the English vanguard had arrived in the Pallinsburn valley. Although the Scots gave up their prepared positions by moving from Flodden Edge and deploying on Branxton Hill, they kept the advantage of the ground and the psychological advantage of meeting their foes without confusion or panic.

When the order was given to move from the camp, the tents, huts and baggage seem to have been left *in situ*, but the gunners had to drag their heavy guns to new positions. Simply moving the guns must have taken a considerable amount of time, and unlike Flodden Edge, where the guns had been pre-sited to cover the main avenues of approach, Robert Borthwick and his gunners did not have much time to select the best firing positions for their pieces. While the position on Flodden Edge had been well prepared, the Scottish army was now launching itself into the unknown. The battle which followed was unplanned and about to be fought on unsurveyed ground. At the very least, this fact removed one of the Scots' greatest advantages.

It is impossible to know the morale within the Scots army during this move but, although the men were bound to have fears and doubts about the coming engagement, the soldiers still had every reason to be confident about the coming battle. The move to Branxton Hill seems to have been accomplished with a minimum of disruption. This was not a desperate manoeuvre forced on the Scots without enough time to carry out the evolution. The Scots still held the high ground, they could see their guns moved into position, and they knew that when the English struggled up the slope towards them, they would be launched down the hill in their pike columns to carry all before them. From the top of Branxton Hill, everything appeared to be in control. There was no reason to worry unduly; through a minor tactical adjustment, James had re-ordered his army and was still in a position to fight the coming battle at an advantage. James IV and his army even now held all the cards.

Once on Branxton Hill, James and his commanders deployed their troops into their positions for the coming engagement. Pitscottie's clearly inaccurate account only mentions two formations; Lord Home and the Earl of Huntly's battle of 10,000 'Borderers and countrymen' and the king's 'great battle'.[80] The only reliable information about the deployment of the Scottish army comes from English observers who were clearly impressed by what they saw. Hall mentions that the Scots were deployed in 'four great battles all on foot with long spears like Moorish pikes', but also states that there were 'two other battles, which never came to hand strokes'.[81] *The Trewe Encountre* agrees that the Scots 'appeared in three great battles'.[82] The *Articules of the Bataille* also gives an obviously eye-witness account:

> The King of Scots army was divided into five battles, and every battle an arrow shot from the other, and all like furnished from the English army in great plumps, part of them quadrant, and some pike wise, and were on the top of the hill, being a quarter of a mile from the foot thereof.[83]

Few of the English soldiers who observed the Scots' deployment would have understood its significance. However, in describing four main formations, 'an arrow shot from the other' massed in 'quadrant' (square) or 'pike wise' (arrow head) 'great plumps', the Lord Admiral was describing the Scots' use of Swiss military methods. In the ensuing account, however, only four Scottish formations are mentioned; that of the Lords Huntly, Erroll and Crawford; the king of Scots; the Earls of Lennox and Argyll; and the Chamberlain, Lord Home.[84] Most subsequent accounts of the battle place the fifth battle, mentioned only once by the *Articules of the Bataille* and not identified further, as under the command of the Earl of Bothwell. However, Bothwell and the 'fifth' battle almost certainly derives from the Italian poem *La Rotta de Scocesi* which identifies both Bothwell and D'Aussi as commanders of separate battles.[85] It is certain that *La Rotta de Scocesi* utilises more than a little poetic licence to ensure that the various nobles engage in individual hand-to-hand combat to add to the drama of the tale and its version of events cannot really be trusted. Hall's two battles which did not come to 'hand strokes' and the *Articules of Bataille's* fifth battle can probably be identified as the Scottish camp followers, horse holders and peasants which followed the army but did not fight. It would appear that the Scottish army was deployed in only four fighting formations.

Although the account states that the Scots were 'on the top of the hill', there is every reason to suggest that the Scots were actually deployed some distance from the crest of Branxton Hill, on the forward slope facing north. When observing north from the geographical crest, vision into the valley below is obscured by the lie of the hill itself. If the Scottish guns had been deployed on the geographical crest, they would not have seen, let alone been able to fire at, the English army. However, 100 yards or so further down the slope, on what is termed the military crest, vision to the north is unobscured. Thus the Scottish army and its guns would have been deployed on the forward slope of Branxton Hill. The Scots artillery would have a clear line of sight to fire at the oncoming English troops, while the men in the pike columns would have seen a smooth but steep descent to their front.

Lord Home's Borderers, armed with the pike, and the Earl of Huntly's Highlanders, armed with their traditional bows, spears and claymores, formed the Scottish vanguard. They were deployed on the forward slope of the western edge of Branxton Hill. It is quite likely that some of Huntly's Gordon clansmen acted as skirmishers, perhaps forming a loose arrowhead formation in front of Home's pikemen, in a mirror of the Swiss methods. 200 yards (an arrow shot) further along the hillside, which was exactly the distance also described by Machiavelli,[86] the Lords Erroll, Crawford and Montrose deployed their men in a large column of pike-men. This body corresponded to the Swiss *gewaltschaufen*. More or less positioned on the centre of the hill, King James IV's 'great battle' was deployed, composed of:

> many bishops, earls, barons, knights and gentlemen of the realm, with a great number of commons.[87]

These formed the rearguard or *nachhut*, according to Swiss practice. The Scots army was deployed in Swiss formation, ready to mount an *echelon* attack, leading from Home and Huntly on the left, on the English army when it appeared. On the Scots' right flank, the Highlanders of Lennox and Argyll were formed up and, while this did not accord with continental military practice, it is clear what their role was intended to be. The lightly armed and equipped Highland troops could not be utilised in the formed pike columns, nor hold a tight formation, so Lennox and Argyll's men were deployed loosely to screen and guard the king's right flank.

As the Scots army came into position on the forward slope of Branxton Hill, the camp followers made fires of the huge piles of straw and rubbish accumulated over the past days by the army. The wet rubbish burnt badly and produced great clouds of smoke, which flowed northwards on the wind. This formed a smokescreen, which concealed the deployment from the English:

> The Scots by their crafty and subtle imagination did set on
> fire all such their filthy straw and litter where as they did lie
> and with the same made such a great and marvellous smoke
> that the manner of their array could not be espied.[88]

There has been much confusion in subsequent accounts of the battle over the nature and purpose of the fires lit by the Scots. It has often been assumed that the fires were started merely to burn the rubbish in the Scottish camp at Flodden Edge, and if this were true, it would be highly unlikely that the fires were used as a deliberate smokescreen. However, the use of fires and smoke to provide concealment had formed part of Scottish military methods since at least the battle of Myton, fought on 20 September 1319.

At Myton, a strong Scottish raiding force, led by the Earl of Douglas, encountered a hastily raised levy of Yorkshire men. Devoid of any properly experienced troops, the English force truly was composed of 'millers and mass priests'. The Scots:

set on fire three stacks of hay; and the smoke thereof was so huge that [the] Englishmen might not see.[89]

The fires produced a thick smokescreen, which covered the Scottish deployment and strength. Due to this concealment, the Scots were able to tempt the English force into a disastrous attack. When the smoke began to clear, the English realised the strength of the Scottish force and began to flee, only to be cut off by Douglas's hard-riding raiders who slaughtered thousands of the English force.[90]

There is no reason to doubt that James ordered a similar smokescreen to cover the deployment of his army on the forward slope of Branxton Hill. This fact is extremely significant. It tells us that James wished to conceal both the size, strength and deployment of his force in an attempt to keep the psychological edge over his opponents, and also confirms that the Scots' march from Flodden Edge was well planned and undertaken in good time. These factors gave the Scots a massive psychological advantage before the battle began.

As the English marched through the rough and broken terrain to the north of Branxton village, their commanders had lost sight of the Scottish army, 'what for the hills and smoke long it was ere the array of the Scots could be conceived'.[91] When the English vanguard crossed the Pallinsburn, and breasted the long southern slope of the Pallinsburn valley, Thomas Howard, the Lord Admiral, rode in front of his men to see if he could observe the Scottish army. He received an enormous shock. It was at this point that the smoke suddenly cleared and 'each army might plainly see one another at hand'. Hall also tells us that:

Both the hosts were very near together within the space of
a quarter of a mile before one of them could perceive
another for the smoke.[92]

To his horror, the admiral could see the entire Scots army
ranged on Branxton Hill in:

four great battles... all on foot with long spears like Moorish
pikes: which the Scots furnished them warlike and bent them
to the forward.[93]

When the two armies came in sight of one another, it was the
Scots who were ready and the English who were dismayed.
Thomas Howard had been ordered to march to the top of
Branxton Hill. The English had hoped that the Scots army
would remain inactive in their camp on Flodden Edge. Instead,
he discovered that the Scots had already redeployed and the
English vanguard was greeted by the soldiers in the first ranks
of the Scottish pike columns who dropped their pikes from
the vertical into their horizontal attacking position.

The admiral was confronted with a terrible situation.
Even his vanguard was still on the march and by no means
ready or deployed for battle. Meanwhile, his men were separated from the rearward by the Pallinsburn bog, and Surrey's
men were still marching to join up with the vanguard. The
admiral no doubt believed that if the Scots attacked now, the
English vanguard, undeployed and fighting alone without
the rearguard, would be routed. But the admiral did not
quite panic. He ordered his men to halt in the Pallinsburn
valley and form up out of sight to give time for the rearward to come up on the left of the vanguard:

> The Lord Howard caused his vaward to stay in a little valley
> till the rearward were joined to one of the wings of his
> battle.[94]

Howard also:

> sent to his father the Earl of Surrey his *agnus dei*★ that hung
> at his breast that in all haste he would join battle, even with
> the brunt or breast of the vanguard, for the forward alone
> was not able to encounter the whole battle of the Scots.[95]

By tearing his medallion from his chest and sending it with
the messenger, Howard certainly impressed his father with
the seriousness of the situation.

When the messenger reached Surrey, he hurried his men
forward. However, in his haste, it would appear that Surrey
gave orders to his own battle and to Dacre, but forgot to
send a messenger to Stanley who was at 'the uttermost part
of the said rearward'.[96] Surrey's men rushed on to join up
with the isolated vanguard, but Stanley was left to march
up to the fight independently. Stanley was probably left
behind without local guides, and his position at the rear of
the line of march may explain why his battle only reached
the field when the majority of the fighting was over.
Eventually, Surrey's men arrived on the field and formed
up on the flank of the vanguard. While the men were forming up, Surrey decided to change his order of battle. He
had organised his men in the traditional English formation
of six units divided between a rearward and vanguard.

★ a 'lamb of God' medallion.

18 Portrait of James IV by Daniel Mytens.

19 Soldiers of Flodden:
Above: English Soldiers: Man at Arms, Professional Soldier, Billman, Border Lance, Longbowman.
Below: Scottish Soldiers: Gentleman, Shire Levy, Borderer, Highland Chieftan, Highland Clansman.

20 Scottish heraldry at Flodden. (From top, left to right): Home, Crawford, King James IV, Erroll, Lennox, Huntly, Montrose, Bothwell, Argyll, Cassillis, Caithness, Crichton, Elphinstone, Erskine, Herries, Marischal, Maxwell, Ross, Rothes, Sempill, Seton.

21 English heraldry. (From top, left to right): Earl of Surrey, Edmund Howard, Thomas Howard, Stanley, Dacre, Constable, Assheton, Booth, Bulmer, Berkeley, Clifford, Cholmondeley, Gower, Lyle, Lumley, Molyneux, Ogle, Savage, Scrope.

22 The 'Flodden Archers' window, St Leonard's Church, Middleton, Lancashire.

Sir Richard Assheton and Dame Anne his wife. anno dñi mccccxxiiij.

23 Drawing of Sir Ralph Assheton and wife as depicted in the window (1845).

24 This coloured engraving of 1845 shows a detail from the complete window. Each kneeling archer has his name inscribed above his bow, with their chaplain, Henry Taylor, extreme right.

Orate pro bono statu Richardi Assheton et eorum qui hanc fenestram fieri fe-

cerunt quorū nōina et imagines ut supra ostenduntur anno dñi mccccxx.

25 Tomb of John, Lord Sempill, who was killed at Flodden, at the Collegiate Church of Castle Semple, Lochwinnoch, which he founded in 1504.

26 Memorial brass epitaph to Sir Marmaduke Constable (d.1518), St Oswald's Church at Flamborough, Yorkshire.

27 *The Death of King James IV.* The King of Scots is cut down yards away from Surrey's banner and his death goes unnoticed in the confusion of battle.

28 *News of Flodden* by William Hole (1902) showing 'Blew Blanket' banner.

29 'The Truth Prevails', bloodstained standard of William Keith, Earl Marischal of Scotland. This banner was concealed and brought home by John Skirving of Plewlandhill, who was captured and imprisoned after the battle.

30 Engraving of the 'Blew Blanket', or 'Craftsman's Banner', said to have been carried by the men of the Incorporated Trades of Edinburgh at the battle. Now kept at the Trades Maidens Hospital, Ashfield, Edinburgh.

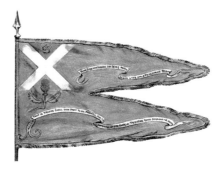

31 Artist's impression of the turquoise ring sent by the queen of France to James IV, and said to have been taken from his body with other battle relics, preserved in the College of Arms, London.

32 Fragment of the St Andrew's Cross, banner of Sir David Home of Wedderburn. He was killed at Flodden by Edmund Howard. This banner is said to have covered the bodies of Sir David and his eldest son when they were brought home after the battle.

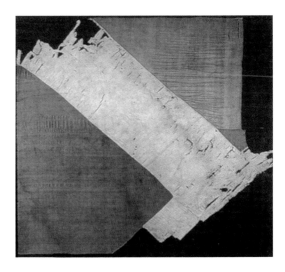

A list of those who fought at Flodden Field in A.D. 1513.

Arncliffe.

John Knolle, able horse and harnish'd. (Armoured)
Oliver Knolle, a bowe.
Robert Tylson, a bille.
William Firth, a bowe.
Richard Clemenger, a bille.
Peter Prass, a bille.
John Carlyll, a bille.
Richard Atkinson, a bowe.
John Wilson, a bowe.
John Atkinson, a bowe.

Hawkswick.

William Calvard, a bowe, able horse &
Arthur Redyman, a bowe, (harnish'd.
  able horse & harnish'd.

33 Illuminated copy of the Flodden List, J.L. Kendall, originally painted on wooden panels in St Oswald's Church, Arncliffe, Yorkshire.

However, Surrey could see that the Scots were in four main formations. If the English did not conform to this deployment, their units might be too small to deal with the massive Scottish pike columns:

> Therefore my Lord Surrey and Lord Howard suddenly were constrained and enforced to divide their army in other four battles, or else it was thought it should have been to their great danger and jeopardy.[97]

Dacre's wing was divided with the Bishop of Ely's men going into Surrey's battle, and some Northumbrians appear to have been sent to Edmund Howard's battle. However, Dacre kept 1,500 Border horse to act as a reserve for the army. Sir Marmaduke Constable's battle was also broken up and most of his men, including his household troops, joined the admiral's battle. This deployment and rearrangement must have been undertaken very hurriedly, which may have caused some confusion amongst the contingents of men. The English army was thus organised into five main units commanded by Edmund Howard, the Lord Admiral, Surrey himself, Lord Dacre and Sir Edward Stanley. Although Surrey had re-organised his formations to match the Scottish deployment, the English battles would still have been linear formations which would be much longer than the deep Scottish pike columns. Once the admiral and earl were satisfied with these alterations, they advanced out of the Pallinsburn valley, 'then both wards in one front advanced against the Scots'.[98]

Meanwhile, the Scots army waited. James has often been criticised for not acting during this period when the English were re-organising their formations (see Map 2). Why did

James not order an all-out attack on the English vanguard while it was isolated and halted in the Pallinsburn valley? The answer is obvious. Had James launched his men down Branxton Hill at this point, his guns would have been left behind and thus useless in the ensuing engagement. Just as importantly, James understood that his pike formations required good ground to be used effectively. Marching forward against an unseen opponent and across steep hills was bound to lead to disorder amongst the Scottish ranks. Further, pike columns were always one-shot weapons. Once they had engaged an enemy force, and hopefully dispersed them, it would be very difficult to re-organise the men to deal with Surrey's rearward. James had no intention of launching a hasty or premature attack on a portion of the English army, which might lead to confusion and uncertainty. He wanted to wait, 'I will have them all before me on a plain field' before starting the engagement.[99] The Scottish guns and pike columns could then be used with maximum effect and hopefully clear the English from the field of battle.

The last and most important point is that, before the opening moves of the battle took place, it is unlikely that James planned to attack. He knew now that the English army had arrived and was deploying for battle. The Scots' deployment had been controlled and their confidence must have soared as they watched the English hurriedly re-organise their formations to conform to the Scots. James probably hoped that the English army would advance to attack him. The Scots artillery would open fire and begin to cause casualties in the English ranks. Eventually, the fire from the vaunted 'seven sisters' would so goad the English that they would attack up Branxton Hill. The English army would toil up the slope

Modern drawing of the *Agnus Dei* emblem, or 'Lamb of God', which appeared on the medallion sent by Thomas Howard, Lord Admiral, to his father, the Earl of Surrey, before the battle.

and become disordered by tiredness and the gaps torn in their ranks by the Scots artillery. Once the English were within good striking range and clearly disorganised, James could order his massive pike columns forward in good order to crush the disordered and disheartened English underfoot. James's inactivity was therefore to good purpose. The English would bring the battle to the Scots and James would then attack and win.

4

THE FIELD OF FLODDEN

Once the English army had advanced onto the low ridge line to the south of Branxton village (marked by Piper's Hill on its western edge), Surrey and the admiral deployed their troops for battle. Edmund Howard's battle took up the right flank, facing Home and Huntly's men. The Lord Admiral's battle, with St Cuthbert's Banner fluttering at its centre, was deployed along the slopes of Piper's Hill, while Surrey's men extended the line in front of Branxton village. Dacre's horsemen formed up behind the admiral and Surrey, acting as a reserve. Stanley's men were still far behind and entirely absent when the battle began. Although Surrey had conformed his deployment to the Scots (there would have been gaps between his battles), the English would have been deployed in much shallower, but wider linear formations than the deep columns of the Scots. As the English positioned their troops along the ridge, the first artillery duel on an English battlefield began. The battle began 'betwixt four and five at after noon'[1] when 'the trumpets blew on every side'[2] and then 'out brast the ordinance on both sides with fire flame and hideous noise'.[3] *The Trewe Encountre* mentions that:

as soon as the Scots perceived my Lords to be within danger of their ordnance they shot sharply their guns which were very great, and in like manner our party recountered them.[4]

However, this artillery duel did not go according to the Scots' plan. Hall tells us that:

the Master Gunner of the English part slew the Master Gunner of Scotland and beat all his men from their ordnance, so that the Scottish ordnance did no harm to the Englishmen.[5]

The Scottish artillery – although modern, well appointed, and certainly formidable looking – did not live up to the high hopes invested in it. Many reasons have been advanced to try and explain this seeming paradox. Hall, in suggesting that the master gunners had 'fought' one another, was simply attempting to personalise the engagement and link it with the tradition of hand-to-hand personal combat. In fact, the 'Master Gunner of Scotland', Robert Borthwick, was not killed at Flodden as he is known to have worked for many years after the battle,[6] but he did have to suffer the agony of seeing his guns fall into English hands. Nonetheless, it is possible that this reference relates to an obviously important Scottish gunner who was seen to fall by the English gunners. Other explanations have suggested that the Scottish guns may have had difficulty in depressing their barrels sufficiently to fire on the English below them, or that they were badly deployed, having been moved in haste from Flodden Edge.

The contemporary accounts cannot tell us the full story of the artillery duel at Flodden mainly because the use of

Guns at the siege of Munster, 1536. This engraving of German guns gives an impression of the appearance of the heavy Scottish guns at Flodden.

artillery was still not fully understood by the gunners of the day, let alone by the chroniclers and commanders who wrote of the engagement. However, it is possible, by understanding the capabilities of the gunpowder artillery of the time, to arrive at a fuller picture of this first British artillery duel.

The main dilemma facing the Scots gunners at Flodden was that the pieces they were serving were superb, modern pieces of heavy siege artillery. Heavy siege guns were well adapted to destroying fortifications, but were at a major disadvantage in field firing. The heavy siege guns had a much slower rate of fire than the light English field guns. Similarly, the Scots gunners were trained and experienced in siege gunnery which emphasised the slow and careful loading of each round to ensure maximum effect against a solid and stationary target. However, in field firing, gunners had to maximise their rate of fire and be trained in the skills of rapid sighting and firing of the gun for maximum effect

Engraving by Durer 1518, which illustrates a light artillery piece, probably a saker. The English falcon guns would have been even lighter than this example.

against a moving target. Without any recoil system, each shot fired by the guns would have resulted in the guns leaping back by several feet.[7] The heavy Scottish guns would have taken considerable effort to manhandle back into position after each shot, an operation which must have slowed the rate of fire yet further.

It is highly unlikely that the Scottish gunners would have had any difficulty in sighting and hitting the English troops. While the slope itself did not hamper the ability of the Scottish gunners to hit their targets, the topography did nonetheless have an important effect. Cannonballs relied for their killing effect not just on hitting their target but on bouncing and ricocheting through their target thus killing far more men. Since the Scots were firing down the slope, the heavy Scottish cannonballs would be likely to burrow themselves into the soft ground, rather than bouncing through the English ranks or gun positions. With a slow rate of fire, and their 'gun stones' hammering into the earth rather than flesh, the Scottish artillery was bound to do relatively little damage. The Scottish gunfire equally had little effect. Leslie lamented that, 'our bullets… did them no hurt, but flew over their heads'.[8]

Meanwhile, the English gunners found themselves in a much more suitable position. The English artillery were light field pieces perfectly suited for battle, and their gunners were trained and experienced in the rapid sighting, loading and firing necessary in battle. The slim, light barrels of the English guns would also have been less prone to overheating, an effect of rapid firing which might well have hampered the Scottish guns. The lighter carriages would also be easier to wheel back into position after each shot, thus increasing their rate of fire relative to the Scots guns. The light English field pieces would also be easily elevated to fire uphill and, since they were firing up a smooth, sloping hill, they were firing their shots onto a perfect surface. The English gunners would have been able to achieve a 'graze' shot so that their cannonballs would hit the ground just in front of the Scottish pike columns and then bounce throughout the depth of the formation, causing heavy casualties.[9]

We should not imagine that the rate of fire, or volume of fire, was impressive by later standards. Nonetheless, the English gunners, with their light field pieces, would have managed to fire two and probably three rounds a minute for a short period of time. The Scottish gunners would have been lucky to have achieved a rate of one shot a minute.[10] It is highly unlikely that the English guns were able to kill or wound all of the Scottish gunners, but it is said that the English fire 'slew the Master Gunner of Scotland and beat all his men from their ordnance'.[11] The English artillery fire probably caused casualties amongst key Scottish gunners, which led to the other gunners running from their guns. We can imagine the Scottish gunners sweating and grunting as they loaded the heavy iron balls into their guns, but soon they must have realised that they were being beaten in the artillery duel. As fast as the Scottish gunners worked, they could not hope to reply effectively with their large and heavy guns, as the more numerous English roundshot came whining through the air at them. The Scottish gunners might well have seemed to be working in slow motion next to the much more rapid evolutions of the English gunners. Once an important gun-captain was killed or wounded, the Scots gunners, completely unprepared for this uneven contest, must have panicked and abandoned their guns.

As the Scottish guns fell silent, the English gunners then turned their attention onto the close-packed ranks of Scottish pikemen. We know that:

> the Englishmen's artillery shot into the midst of the King's battle and slew many persons.[12]

Even though the English falcons were firing cannonballs only 2 inches in diameter, they could have an enormous impact on such a large target as a pike column of perhaps 9,000 men. Even by the eighteenth and nineteenth centuries, artillery fire was not necessarily devastating. But at close range, and firing into a large stationary target, artillery fire could cause serious casualties. Given the size of the target, the English gunners did not even need to be particularly accurate. Once they had found the range, almost every shot would be bound to tumble through the length of the ranks of Scottish soldiers, causing horrific injuries and dis-ordering the close-packed ranks of men. Each roundshot which hit a pike column could have cut down at least four or five men. With the English artillery cutting gaps in the Scots ranks, King James IV faced a situation that he had never expected. He had to think and act quickly to save his army from confusion and panic. There were a number of options open to James which are easy to consider in the calm of hindsight, but which were not so easy to review on the battlefield amongst the screams of wounded men and the smell of powder smoke.

Although King James and his men were experiencing the results of the first artillery duel in British military history, their experience would later be repeated throughout the centuries down to the present day. The English guns could kill at much greater ranges than any of the more traditional weapons which were present at Flodden. While the English longbowmen could kill at a maximum of 300 yards range, and quite probably less at Flodden due to the wind and rain, the English artillery were firing at perhaps 600 yards range. Even though the Scots were well outside what had been the danger distance on medieval battlefields, 300 yards or extreme longbow shot, they were now being cut down at perhaps twice that distance. There was also literally nothing that a Scottish soldier in a pike column could do against an artilleryman firing a gun 600 yards away. While the Scots soldiers would want to advance and fight the English or get away from the danger, while standing in their close-packed formations they could do nothing. James could have held his men in their ranks and hoped that the English artillery fire would slacken as the gunners got tired, before too much damage had been sustained. However, simply standing on Branxton Hill would do nothing to force an engagement because, with the loss of his own artillery, James could no longer goad the English into an attack.

An equally unattractive option would have been to order his army to retire behind the crest of Branxton Hill. This would have protected the army from the English artillery fire and forced the English to attack. However, such a move would have been far too risky. An order for a retreat while the troops were under fire would almost certainly have been interpreted as defeat. In the ensuing disorder and confusion, the Scottish troops might well have dissolved into panic and rout.

The only other option for James was to order his troops to march down the slopes of Branxton Hill and attack the English army immediately. James could hope that his pike columns would sweep away the English army before the English guns could do any more damage. Thus, in this extremely stressful situation, James and his army really had only two choices: fight or flight. In fact, ordering an advance against the English was not only a logical decision, but was also enshrined in Scottish military practice. The Scots at Flodden were not used to facing an artillery bombardment, but Scottish armies for the past 200 years had been faced with the storm of arrows shot by English longbowmen. On each and every occasion, Scottish armies had attempted to close the range and enter hand-to-hand combat as quickly as possible to decide the battle and to prevent further casualties from missile fire.[13] Indeed, most Renaissance armies acted in a similar fashion. The Swiss were noted for their rapid advance on the battlefield, particularly when they were brought under artillery fire. It was recognised by Renaissance military commanders that to stand stationary under artillery bombardment was the worst possible option. This dilemma had recently wrecked the Spanish army at Ravenna and, as Machiavelli commented:

> It is certain that small pieces of cannon… do more damage than heavy artillery. The best remedy against the latter is making a resolute attack upon it as soon as possible; if you lose some of your men in so doing [which must always be the case], surely a partial loss is not so bad as a total defeat. The Swiss are worthy of imitation in this respect; they never decline an engagement out of fear of artillery, but always give the death penalty to those who would stir from their ranks, or show the least sign of being frightened by it.[14]

Thus, in a matter of minutes, the whole course of the battle had changed. The Scots had hoped that their artillery fire would goad the English into a premature assault, but now it was the Scots who had to attack. James had been forced to throw away his previous battle plan and risk everything in an all-out attack. We are told by Hall that, observing the damage the English artillery was causing:

> the King of Scots and his noble men, made the more haste to come to joining, and so all the four battles in manner descended the hill at once.[15]

The Trewe Encountre agrees that:

> our guns did so break and constrain the Scottish great army that some part of them were enforced to come down toward our army.[16]

The English chroniclers agree that it was their artillery fire which precipitated the advance of the Scottish army – and indeed it had. We know that Home and Huntly's vanguard was the first to engage the English army, and it has often been argued that the Borderers and Highlanders could stand the bombardment no longer and began a spontaneous attack without orders. King James has also often been criticised for leaving his army without orders, and for fighting an unplanned and uncontrolled battle.

However, these arguments misunderstand the true nature of the Scottish deployment and the subsequent advance. We know that the Scots:

> came down the hill and met with them in good order after the Almayns manner without speaking of any word.[17]

Machiavelli discussed the advantages of maintaining silence in the ranks before actual contact:

> The opinions of ancient authors vary concerning this matter, whether those beginning the battle should rush on with furious shouts and outcries, or march up to the attack with silence and composure. The latter is certainly the most proper means of preserving good order, and of hearing commands most distinctly... But I do not think a continual shout can be of any service; quite the contrary, it will prevent the general's orders from being heard – this must be attended with terrible consequences.[18]

We can be sure that the Scottish vanguard did not make an uncontrolled advance. Troops driven to distraction under artillery fire would have been badly rattled, and no doubt shouting their defiance and rage at the English. Instead, they made a disciplined and controlled advance towards their English enemies 600 yards away.

In fact, it is quite clear why the Scottish vanguard started down the hill first. The Scots were attacking 'after the Almayns manner', in an *echelon* formation. To an English observer, more accustomed to a linear advance by an army, this diagonal attack may well have been confusing. From the Scots' perspective, the intention would have been very clear. The Scottish advance and attack would take place in sequence, steadily increasing the pressure on the English line. Home and Huntly's vanguard would lead the attack, closely followed by the column of Erroll, Crawford and Montrose, while the 'great battle' or rearguard of the king would then complete the victory.

This surely explains the slightly confusing meaning of the English accounts which state that:

> All these four battles, in manner fought at one time, and were determined in effect, little in distance of the beginning and ending of any one of them before the other, saving that Sir Edward Stanley which was the last that fought.[19]

and also that 'so all the four battles in manner descended the hill at once'.[20] This would seem conclusive evidence that, when the Scots army started down the hill, it did so in the diagonal *echelon* formation, *en masse* and under control.

Once James had given the order to attack, and with his nobles clear on their orders and formation of attack, there was little more he could do as a commander. The Scottish pike columns could only march straight forward in formation towards their respective targets. Pike columns were not subtle weapons. There could be no thought of a change in formation or direction, let alone a retreat, once the order to advance was given. The Scots pikemen would either push forward and win, or they would be halted and lose. It is perhaps significant that the Swiss never developed a proper chain of command within their armies. There was no real commander-in-chief beyond an elected old soldier who exercised no real command function. The tactics and formation to be used in battle were worked out by a committee of captains in a council of war before the battle.[21] In action, each Swiss formation operated more or less independently. With his role as commander-in-chief seemingly complete, James picked up a pike and walked to the front rank of his own formation to lead it into battle. He believed that his personal leadership would give his army the momentum necessary to win. His nobles protested but his mind was made up. He was going to lead his men to victory.

Even in the twenty-first century, the debate about the correct position, role and place for a commander-in-chief to take in battle goes on. Sir Douglas Haig, the Commander-in-Chief of the British Expeditionary Force from 1916–18, has often been criticised (perhaps unfairly) for his remote style of command.[22] Meanwhile, commanders such as Field Marshal Erwin Rommel, commander of the *Panzerarmee Afrika* in North Africa during the Second World War, who often shared the risks of his men and inspired them by leading from the front, have been applauded.[23] Such a debate would have been meaningless to James IV of Scotland. He knew that personal leadership was essential; he must place 'himself the first in danger'.[24]

In leading from the front, James was merely acting in accordance with Scottish custom and the demands of medieval kingship. For at least a century, Scots nobles had stiffened the front ranks of their *schiltrons* by leading from the front. Equipped with the best armour and weapons, the Scots nobles and their retainers provided a sharp cutting edge to the mass of levies, which marched behind them. James was simply taking his place as the 'Great Captain' in front of his troops. There is little doubt that his men's morale would have soared when they saw James and his Royal Standard in the front rank. The soldiers, gentry and nobles must have felt that their king would lead them to victory.

Once the king's battle began to move, with the battle led by Erroll, Crawford and Montrose 200 yards to their left, and Home and Huntly's vanguard all on the march down the hill, the Scottish army must have been an impressive and awe-inspiring sight. The king's battle, with perhaps as many as 9,000 men, would have been twenty ranks deep and have 450 men in each rank. The heavily armed and armoured nobles took up the front ranks and presented a mass of pike points towards the English. It was noted that many of the Scots had taken off their shoes and fought in the 'vamps of their hose'[25] to gain grip on the muddy slopes of Branxton Hill. This was a tradition amongst Scots pikemen and had been noted by English chroniclers as early as the battle of the Standard in 1138.

As the Scots came down the slope in silence, no doubt halting at intervals to 'dress' their ranks to keep order, the English guns continued to fire on these moving masses of men. Once the Scots had marched 300 paces down Branxton Hill, the cannonballs of the English artillery were joined by the arrow storm fired from the English longbows. While the artillery's roundshot must have ploughed gaps in their ranks, the English archers did not have their traditional effect. Since the battle of Falkirk in 1298, English and Welsh longbow-men had brought disaster to Scottish armies of spearmen. Yet in its last major battle on British soil, the much-vaunted longbow was ineffective. The chroniclers give two main reasons for this disappointing result. The first relates to the weather, as 'there was great wind and sodden rain, all contrary to our bows and archers'.[26] The heavy rain dampened the bowstrings which reduced the pulling power of the bows, while the wind blew the arrows off target. However, the environmental conditions only contributed to the archers' failure. The main problem for the English archers was that:

> The Scots were so surely harnessed with complete harness, German jacks, rivets, splents, pavises and other habiliments, that shot of arrows in regard did them no harm.[27]

Another account admits that:

> They were so well appointed… with arms and harness… that few of them were slain with arrows.[28]

It was also said that the Scots shielded themselves against the arrows by carrying 'Pavises'.[29] Pavises were large wooden shields which had been designed by the French to protect their soldiers from the English arrow storm, which had killed so many Frenchmen on battlefields from Crécy to Agincourt. While the lavish equipment and armour protected the front ranks of the Scottish phalanxes from the volleys of arrows, the forest of raised pikes would also give some protection to the men in the middle and rear of the formation. Finally, after 200 years, the Scots had found the answer to the English longbow. The English archers must have been dismayed to see the Scots close the range without their archery having any appreciable effect. Flodden, unlike Halidon Hill, Homildon Hill or Falkirk was not begun and ended by a storm of English arrows, but would, just as the Scots had intended, be decided by close combat or 'hand strokes'.

Home and Huntly's vanguard was the first to clash with the English and certainly had the greatest impact of all the Scottish units. Home, with his Border pikemen, and Huntly, with his Gordon clansmen armed with axes, claymores and bows, advanced across relatively open terrain towards the small battle of Edmund Howard. With an unobstructed march towards the English, Home and Huntly's men pushed straight on to the English formation. The Scottish pikemen rolled over the English position and this caused panic amongst Edmund Howard's men:

> the Cheshire and Lancashire men never abode stroke and few of the gentlemen of Yorkshire abode but fled.[30]

The *Scotish Feilde* describes the fight graphically:

> they proched us with spears and put many over, that the blood out burst at their broken harness.[31]

Due to the open terrain, and the ability of the Scots to hold their formation as they advanced, Home and Huntly's formation won exactly the kind of success that pikes were designed to achieve. Pitscottie tells us that:

> the Earl of Huntly's Highland men with their bows and two-handed swords fought so manfully that they defeated the Englishmen.[32]

Huntly's Highlanders, armed with the fearsome two-handed sword or claymore, may well have acted in the same manner as the *dopplensolders* of the *landsknechts*, by opening up gaps in the English ranks and leaving them hopelessly vulnerable to the advance of Home's pikemen. Presented with an impenetrable mass of pike points inexorably advancing towards them, the English soldiers could neither reach the Scottish soldiers with their swords and bills, nor could they hold their ground and absorb the impact of the relentless Scottish advance. If the English soldiers remained where they stood, they would be knocked down by the Scottish pikes creating chaos and confusion. Not surprisingly, unable to hold their ground or fight effectively, most of the men simply ran:

> *then betide a check that Cheshire men fledden*
> *when the Scots and Cattericks seen our men scatter*
> *they had great joy of their joining and jollily*
> *came downward.*[33]

The poem also attempts to explain away the rout by referring to feudal loyalty. The Cheshire and Lancashire men had been separated from the formation led by Sir Edward Stanley. Uncertain of Edmund Howard's leadership since, 'they were wont at all wars to wait upon the Stanleys',[34] they had fled at the Scots' advance. However, the real reason lay in the tactical problem that confronted the English soldiers.

As the front ranks of the English line buckled and broke as men were knocked over or tried to run, we can only imagine the chaos as the noblemen tried to keep their men together. Soon only a few clumps of men were left around Edmund Howard and some of his nobles, who stood their ground. Bryan Tunstall of Thurland knelt down to take a piece of earth into his mouth as a last Communion before killing a Scots knight and then being cut down himself. Maurice Berkeley was also killed while Christopher Savage, the Mayor of Macclesfield who had fought at Bosworth in 1485, died along with most of his men. The hard knots of English defenders were either killed or scattered by the points of the Scottish pikes, and Edmund Howard was soon surrounded and isolated with his standard bearer and two servants. Howard's standard was taken and his standard bearer 'beaten and hewed in pieces'.[35] Howard himself was knocked to the ground three times by Borderers who wanted to take him prisoner for ransom, but he managed to get back up each time, lashing out with his sword. By this time, Home and Huntly's close formation had dissolved and there would have been numerous individual fights between the Scots and surviving English.

At this critical point, Lord Dacre came to Edmund Howard's rescue with his 1,500 Border horsemen. It is not known whether he was ordered by Surrey or whether he acted on his own initiative, but Dacre's intervention certainly saved Surrey's son from capture. With the fighting now fragmented into individual mêlées, the Scots were in no position to resist a charge by Dacre's horsemen. Bastard John Heron and a small party of men managed to cut their way through the press of men and reached Edmund Howard. Heron himself was badly wounded during the rescue attempt:

> came John Heron, Bastard sore hurt, saying there was never a noble man's son so like to be lost as you be on this day, for all my hurts I will here lie and die with you.[36]

These were brave words from a man whose murder of Sir John Kerr had been one of the Scottish grievances before the war, but Heron and Howard somehow managed to cut their way through to safety. At one point, their path was blocked by Sir David Home of Wedderburn, the brother of Lord Home, but Edmund Howard cut him down and managed to reach the admiral's battle.

Meanwhile a vicious fight went on between Home and Huntly's men and Dacre's horsemen. Dacre lost at least 160 men and three notable men, Philip Dacre, Sir Humphrey Lisle and Henry Gray, were all captured by the Scots. Nonetheless, a 'great number of Scots were slain'.[37] Three of Home's cousins were killed along with many Border gentry and lairds, and Huntly's contingent suffered the loss of at least four Gordon chieftains.

Eventually, both sides drew apart. At some point Home and Huntly, 'blew their trumpets and convened their men again to their standards'.[38] Both sides must have attempted to rally their men back to their standards and regain control

Woodcut from John Skelton's *A Ballade of the Scottysshe Kynge*: This
shows a fully armoured horseman wearing a German-style sallet, and
a Border horseman or 'pricker' wearing a jack or brigandine.

over their dispersed and bloodied soldiers. Neither the Scots
nor the English on this part of the field continued to play
an active part in the battle. Dacre's men were eventually
rallied and held their ground on the right flank of the admiral's battle. Many writers have suggested that this disengage-
ment amounted to a Border truce, as was common amongst
Borderers at the time. Pitscottie relates that later in the battle,
when it was clear that the king's battle was hardpressed,
Huntly begged Home to go to the king's aid. Home replied
that:

He does well that does for himself: we have fought our
vanguard already and won the same therefore let the rest do
their part as well as we.[39]

Home's supposed failure to help the king at Flodden was
certainly one of the rumours which hung around the
Chamberlain until his execution for treason in 1516.[40]
However, both the trial and Pitscottie's account were heavily biased against a man who had sided with the English
since James IV's death, and such accusations were not necessarily truthful. Given the heavy casualties sustained on
both sides, it is likely that both the Scots and English on this
flank were fought out and incapable of indulging in more
fighting. Neither Home nor Dacre would have been able to
rouse their men for more effort when the battle had already
been decided. Nonetheless, Home and Huntly had achieved
considerable success but, with Dacre's intervention, the most
dangerous Scottish onslaught had eventually been held in
check. Home and Huntly seem to have rallied their men as
best they could and then withdrawn from the field when
they observed the disaster in the centre.

The fight between Home, Huntly, Edmund Howard and
Lord Dacre was certainly bloody but inconclusive, and it
was in the centre of the field that the battle would be
decided. Within minutes of the Scottish vanguard becoming
engaged, the phalanx led by Erroll, Crawford and Montrose
must have crashed into the Lord Admiral's battle. However,
neither their men, nor the king's battle, encountered the
same smooth ground that had contributed to Home and
Huntly's success. At the bottom of Branxton Hill there is a
small boggy stream which, like the Pallinsburn, is little more

than a 'man's step over',[41] but this insignificant watercourse had a fatal effect on the Scottish columns which had to cross it. While Edmund Howard's men had been posted on a level plain, the troops of the Lord Admiral and the Earl of Surrey were deployed on a low ridge, which rose on the other side of the stream. Unfortunately for James, this small stream was virtually imperceptible from the top of Branxton Hill. James's decision to launch his men in an assault was probably made without realising the existence of the stream or the disastrous effect it could have on the order of his formations. It meant that his men would have to negotiate their way across a small stream with the English army waiting for them on higher ground less than 100 yards away.

The Scots pike phalanxes would have been able to keep their order and formation all the way down Branxton Hill until they encountered the small stream but, as the front ranks scrambled across, the order and cohesion of the force (so essential for success) would have dissolved. As the front ranks struggled to regain their order on the far side of the stream, the rest of the pikemen would bunch up as they waited to cross. Combined with the last salvoes of artillery and arrows from the English army, the little stream would have thrown the Scottish columns into disorder and confusion. As the Scots advanced to within closing distance, the English archers would loose off their last arrows and then move to the rear of the English formations. Once the archers had passed through their ranks, the billmen would then have closed up into a tighter formation ready to meet the Scottish advance.

Instead of pushing onto the waiting English troops in good order, presenting a wall of pike points to the English line, the Scots columns suffered a fatal loss of momentum.

The column of Erroll, Montrose and Crawford seems to have been particularly affected by the 'unevenness of the hill'.[42] The admiral's battle was deployed around Piper's Hill, a considerable eminence on the western edge of the ridge. The men of Erroll, Crawford and Montrose's column were badly disordered by the stream and then tired by the effort of climbing Piper's Hill. Robbed of their momentum and the order vital to the success of a pike phalanx attack, the Scots formation had lost the power to roll over the English to their front. Instead, the admiral's division was able to absorb the impact of the Scots' advance and bring the pike column to a halt. Once halted and disordered, the power of the Scots pike column evaporated into a tangle of individual men struggling to wield their unhandy pikes. It was this break-up of the Scots formation which gave the English billmen their chance.

The English soldiers must have been badly frightened by the onset of the Scottish columns. Some of them may well have witnessed the rout of Edmund Howard's battle on their right, and they would have been only too aware that they too could suffer a similar fate if the Scots were able to regain their order and formation. The English billmen grabbed the only opportunity they had to fight and win. The initial period of contact would have resulted in some 'fencing' by the billmen as they attempted to clear the Scottish pikes out of the way so that they could get in close enough to the Scots to wield their bills effectively.[43] As the English pushed forwards and came to 'hand strokes', the fighting dissolved into individual hand-to-hand combat, where the 18-foot pikes carried by the Scots were simply a liability. Once at close quarters the English billmen had the advantage. The billmen, with their 8-foot-long shaft that carried a billhook, point and blade, could exploit the gaps in the Scottish formation, chop off the heads of the Scottish pikes, or thrust them aside and then slash and tear at the pikemen themselves.

Just as the men of Erroll, Crawford and Montrose, who had toiled up Piper's Hill, began to get into difficulty, the king's battle must have crossed the stream and surged forwards up the slope into the waiting ranks of the Earl of Surrey's battle. James, surrounded by the 'most part of the noble men of his realm',[44] managed to drive the English back by perhaps as much as 200 yards, but his column, also disordered by the small stream, did not have the momentum to break the cohesion of Surrey's men. The battle here also came to 'hand strokes' with the English billmen wading into the gaps in the Scottish ranks.

One English writer remarked that, 'Our bills... disappointed the Scots of their long spears wherein was their greatest trust'.[45] The Italian poem *La Rotta de Scocesi* described this:

> *You saw so many weapons lowered that it seemed as if a wood were falling down.*[46]

Indeed, there must have been a rippling effect all along the line as the Scots dropped their pikes and drew their swords, axes, mallets or whatever other secondary weapons they possessed. Another witness stated that:

> And when their spears failed and were spent, then they fought with great and sharp swords.[47]

The Scots had placed 'their greatest trust' in a weapons system that failed at the critical moment. At the same time, the longer, more linear formation adopted by the English would have meant that, when the Scottish columns came into contact, the front ranks of the English billmen would overlap the Scots formations. The Scots pikemen on the flanks of their formation soon found themselves fighting to their front and side against numerous English billmen. Although well armoured and armed, the Scots now had to fight at a terrible disadvantage. Just as the Scottish pikes had outreached the English bills, so now the bills could outreach the Scottish swords:

> and when they came to hand stroke, though the Scots fought sore and valiantly with their swords, yet they could not resist the bills that lighted so thick and so sore upon them.[48]

It was said that 'the battle was cruel' and it must have been a grim fight with both sides hacking and slashing at each other. While the Scots would have attempted to parry the bills and somehow land a killing blow on their English enemies who were now out of their reach, the billmen would have used their pole-arm to snatch at the knees, jab at the face or land a crushing blow to the helmet of their opponent in an attempt to knock him off his feet. Once knocked down, the heavily armoured Scottish soldier, if not trampled underfoot, could be despatched easily. The bill was indeed a cruel weapon which could butcher an opponent. It was during this fierce, but unequal, struggle that the morale of the Scots must have broken.

Ardant du Picq, a French infantry officer who was killed in the Franco-Prussian War of 1870, was the first writer to attempt to analyse the psychology of soldiers in battle. While du Picq was interested in whether the deep attack column of the Napoleonic era was obsolete in the 1860s, his observations about the psychology at work in columns and pike phalanxes do have relevance for Flodden. Du Picq studied ancient warfare and the pike phalanxes of the Greeks and Alexander the Great. He noted that when an attack by men in a column or phalanx met with difficulty: 'demoralization and flight began in the rear ranks'.[49]

The noblemen and their retainers, who made up the front ranks of the Scottish columns, had no choice but to drop their pikes, draw their swords and continue to fight. They knew that they were now fighting at a disadvantage but could do nothing to turn the tide in their favour. The pikes had failed them and they had not rolled over the English as their French advisors had told them they would. This was not a modern continental 'technological' battle anymore but a vicious fight with the 'auld enemy'.

The Scots noblemen and their supporters had not come to Branxton Hill to be butchered by English billmen, their social inferiors, but to win a glorious victory. The fighting was fierce and grim with 'many onsets, muckle slaughter, sweating and travail'.[50] The Scots in the front ranks fought on in silence:

It is not to be doubted but the Scots fought manfully, and were determined either to win the field or die.[51]

While the Scots soldiers in the middle of the phalanx 'could scarcely see and even the first two lines hardly had a free position for striking',[52] the men at the back and on the edges

Engraving by Hans Burgkmaier of the battle of Flodden, which illustrates the fighting and rout of the Scots. King James IV is shown lying dead in the foreground.

of the columns were in a very different position. They saw the forest of pikes in front of them fall, and they would realise very quickly that the battle was no longer going according to plan or in their favour. The men in the rear ranks of the Scottish columns were the least well equipped and armoured, and probably with the least combat motivation. These men were almost certainly poor farm hands and labourers with little conception of what they were fighting for. With their feudal superiors packed into the front ranks, these men lacked the presence of the leaders, which they needed to steady their shaken confidence in this terrifying situation. The Scots in the rear ranks of the columns were not held in their places by the fierce collective discipline present in the Swiss columns and when these ordinary men witnessed some of the carnage going on in front of them, and realised that their feudal leaders were being butchered by the English billmen, some of them must have panicked and started to run. Du Picq states that:

> The contagion of fear changes the direction of the human wave; it bends back upon itself and breaks to escape danger.[53]

The rear ranks of both Scottish columns at some point broke and ran. The *Articules of the Bataille* state that 'shortly their backs were turned',[54] yet the fighting at the front of the Scottish columns continued. Most accounts of the fighting suggest that the admiral's battle and Sir Edward Stanley's men moved in on the flanks and rear of the king's battle, thus trapping the Scots in an unequal fight. It is much more likely that, since each fight was decided at roughly the same time, and given the enormous difficulties in manoeuvring troops over the chaos of a battlefield, the sequence of events was somewhat different. When the rear ranks of the Scottish columns ran from the fight, and with the English billmen fighting with the Scottish front ranks, the English archers from each English formation, who had stood behind the billmen, would have flowed round the struggling mass of men to envelop the Scots in the flank and rear as well as pursue the Scots who were fleeing the fight.

The Scots of Erroll, Crawford and Montrose's column had aimed for St Cuthbert's Banner held aloft in the centre of the admiral's battle, but:

> they got no advantage but great loss and damage of their folks; and yet few or none being under the same banner were slain, though many hurt.[55]

All three earls were killed along with many men from the eastern Lowlands. Eighty-seven Hays died alongside Errol, the head of their family.[56]

As the fighting turned against the Scots, James made a last ditch effort to win the battle. Gathering his household around him, James led them in a final charge towards Surrey's banners:

> He rushed into the chiefest press of his enemies, and there fighting in a most desperate manner was beaten down and slain.[57]

King James IV of Scotland 'was slain within a spear length from the said Earl of Surrey' and his banner. James had almost reached his personal target when, surrounded by English billmen, he was hacked down.

In the confusion and press of the fighting, the king's death went unnoticed and the grim and unequal contest continued. Now outnumbered by the English billmen and archers who surrounded them, the front ranks of the Scottish columns were hacked to pieces. Bishop Ruthal wrote that:

when it come to hand strokes of bills and halberds they were so mighty, large, strong and great men that they would not fall when four or five bills struck on one of them at once.[58]

A terrible picture emerges of heavily armoured Scottish soldiers beating off numerous billmen, but who eventually succumbed to repeated attacks. The battlefield turned into a butcher's yard, as individual heavily armoured Scots noblemen lashed out at the mass of billmen who 'beat and hew them down'[59] to the ground. This fight was not without 'pain and danger to Englishmen,'[60] many of whom must have been wounded in this close fight. But while an injured English billman might push his way to safety, the Scots were trapped. Once wounded or knocked on the ground, the Scots were killed.

With terrible irony, the English now utilised the only Swiss method that counted; true to the admiral's word, they took no prisoners. *The Trewe Encountre* tells us that:

> Many other Scottish prisoners could and might have been taken but they were so vengeable and cruel in their fighting that when the Englishmen had the better of them they would not save them, though it so were that diverse Scots offered great sums of money for their lives.[61]

Perhaps as few as 400 Scots were taken prisoner by the English. The vast majority were simply slaughtered on the field. Bishop Ruthal noted that:

34 Thomas Howard, 3rd Duke of Norfolk, who as Lord Admiral of England, commanded the vanguard of the English army at Flodden.

35 Twizzell Bridge, over which Thomas Howard's vanguard marched on the morning of the battle.

36 Memorial brass to Sir William Molyneux (d.1548) and his two wives in Sefton, Lancashire. It includes images of two Scottish banners, captured by Molyneux at Flodden (bottom right).

37 Branxton Village from Branxton Hill (above) and Piper's Hill, taken from the approximate position of James IV's battle. The low ridge runs from Piper's Hill to the south of the village.

38 Branxton Hill taken from the English ridge, showing the smooth, steep slope on which the Scottish army began the battle. Home and Huntly's men were deployed on the right, Erroll, Crawford and Montrose in the centre and King James IV's battle on the left.

39 This shows the western edge of Branxton Hill and the slopes over which Home and Huntly's men advanced in the middle distance. Edmund Howard's battle was routed in this area.

40 The small stream and ditch which lie at the bottom of Branxton Hill. The English ridge can be seen to the right. This insignificant watercourse had a major impact on the nature of the battle.

41 Effigies of Sir Richard Cholmondeley and his wife at St Peter Ad Vincula, Tower of London. He was knighted for his service at Flodden and became Lieutenant of the Tower of London. He died in 1544.

42 Engraving of a sword and dagger, said to have been carried by James IV at Flodden, now in the College of Arms, London.

43 Branxton Church and village. The church was used as a mortuary after the battle.

44 Remains of the Collegiate Church, Castle Semple, Lochwinnoch, Renfrewshire, which contains the memorial tomb of John, Lord Sempill, who was killed at Flodden. The tomb is perhaps the only contemporary Scottish memorial to one of the dead at Flodden.

45, 46 The Howard family arms with the Flodden augmentation proudly displayed in stone on the Fitzroy tomb at Framlingham, Suffolk; and in glass at Barham Hall.

47 The Flodden Wall at Edinburgh.

48 The Selkirk statue of Fletcher by Thomas Clapperton. He was reputed to be the sole survivor of the Selkirk contingent of eighty men sent to Flodden. He bears the captured banner of Sir Christopher Savage's Macclesfield company.

Our folks intending to make all things sure took little regard in taking of prisoners, but rid all that came to hand, both King, bishops, lords, knights, nobles or others whatsoever came which were not so soon slain but forthwith despoiled out of their harness and array and left lying naked in the field.[62]

Very soon after the fight had ended, the only Scots left on the field were captives or dead.

While the struggle in the centre of the battle reached its climax, the last fight at Flodden began. Sir Edward Stanley's battle was 'the uttermost part of the said rearward'[63] and arrived late on the battlefield. We are told that:

And in the time of this battle [between King James and Surrey] the Earls of Lennox and Argyll, with their puissaunces, joined with Sir Edward Stanley, and they were put to flight.[64]

This suggests that there was still some fighting going on when Stanley first appeared on the field. Stanley must have seen the fighting in the centre, but he also saw the Highlanders of Lennox and Argyll still standing in position on top of Branxton Hill. Thinking that the Highlanders posed a real danger and were 'ready to relieve the said King of Scots battle',[65] Stanley decided to climb the hill and attack them. Certainly, Lennox and Argyll did not make any offensive moves during the battle, and this has often been ascribed to James's failure to give them any orders (see Map 4). In fact, by remaining on Branxton Hill, the Highlanders were still fulfilling an important function. They were guarding the Scottish artillery and still providing flank protection to the king's battle down in the valley. Stanley, when he arrived, could not put his force into the struggle around Surrey's banners because if he had done so, the Highlanders could have hit him in the rear. Instead, Stanley's powerful force had to be used against the supporting Highlanders rather than becoming involved in the main fight.

Stanley's men advanced towards Branxton Hill from the northeast where the slopes are very steep, and where his men could toil up the hill hidden from the view of Argyll and Lennox on the hilltop. The climb was so steep that:

> *His folks could scarcely fast their feet*
> *But forced on hands and feet to creep*
> *… At last the mountain top they wan.*[66]

Stanley's men managed to reach the crest of the hill before the Highlanders were even aware of their approach. Once in range, Stanley's Lancashire and Cheshire longbowmen loosed off flights of arrows into the Highland ranks. These arrows took deadly effect on the unarmoured clansmen who were also surprised by the sudden onslaught. Panicked by the arrow storm, the Highlanders put up little resistance when Stanley's billmen charged into their disordered ranks. Both earls (along with many of their closest kinsmen) were killed as they attempted to steady their men, but most of the Highlanders panicked and ran. The Highlanders seem to have run down Branxton Hill, probably because they were taken in the rear and flank by Stanley's men and fled across the site of struggle between the Earl of Surrey and King James which had, by now, reached its bloody conclusion. Stanley's men pursued the Scots:

over the same ground, where the Earl's battle slain before, and suddenly left the chase and fell a spoiling, and spoiled the King of Scots, and many that were slain in his battle, but they knew him not.[67]

Just as Stanley's men fell to plundering the dead, so too must many of the rest of the English force. The promise of real riches lying in the mud before them would have been a powerful incentive. Although many of the English soldiers plundered the dead on the battlefield, others pursued the fleeing Scots:

> many Englishmen followed them into Scotland, and were so far that they wist not which way to return and so were taken prisoners of the Scots.[68]

The *Articules of the Bataille* claims that 'the chase continued three miles with marvellous slaughter',[69] but it is unclear which units were able to pursue the routed Scots and which remained to slaughter and plunder the Scottish noblemen. However, the *Scotish Feilde* also boasts that:

> *then they fettled them to fly as fast as they might,*
> *but that served not, for soothe, who so truth telleth.*
> *Our Englishmen full eagerly after them followed,*
> *And killed them like cattle in valleys all about.*[70]

While Pitscottie claimed that the battle ended with neither side certain of victory, and that the English army remained under arms on the field that night, there is little doubt that Flodden ended with a limited English pursuit of the fleeing remnants of the Scottish army.

As night fell, both armies were scattered over a wide area. Most of the survivors of the Scottish army were running headlong for the border, while evading a largely imaginary English pursuit:

> Of the Scots that fled some passed over the water of Tweed at Coldstream ford, and other by the dry marches, during the time of the fight.[71]

Only Lord Home and the Earl of Huntly had managed to rally at least some of their men and draw them off the field in some order. Some English soldiers were fortunate enough to find their way to the Scottish camp on Flodden Edge. In amongst the tents, the soldiers found:

> plenty of wine, beer, ale, beef, mutton, salt fish, cheese and other vitals necessary and convenient for such a great army.

This certainly suggests that the Scots army was well provisioned, but some English soldiers:

> doubting that the said vitals had been poisoned for their destruction, would not save but utterly them destroyed.[72]

Bishop Ruthal's men seem not to have been quite so fussy about the Scottish supplies, and drank much of the beer 'to their great refreshing'.[73]

Surrey kept as many men as he could together under his banners and sent out scouts to discover if all of the Scots had fled the area:

Woodcut from John Skelton's *A Ballade of the Scottysshe Kynge*, showing the Earl of Surrey in the Scottish camp after the battle, receiving James IV's crown.

When the field was done and the scout watch brought word that there was no more appearance of the Scots, but all were returned. The Earl thanked God with humble heart, and called to him certain lords and other gentlemen and them made knights as Sir Edmond Howard his son and the Lord Scrope, Sir William Percy and many other.[74]

Surrey knighted a total of forty gentlemen[75] on the field that night, before returning with his son, the Lord Admiral, to the camp at Barmoor where the Lord Admiral dashed off a quick despatch of the victory, which was immediately sent to Queen Katherine. Surrey ordered Sir Phillip Tylney to gather the companies of the Lord Admiral, Lord Scrope, Sir Marmaduke Constable, Sir William Percy and Sir Nicholas Appleyard's gunners and keep them under arms on the field

of battle: for 'saving of the English ordnance, and the ordnance that was taken from the Scots'.[76] This gives a very
good indication that the companies of the other English
captains must have been dispersed and impossible to rally
that night. The English companies which remained under
arms on the battlefield guarding the ordnance must surely
be the root of Pitscottie's claim that the English army:

> stood on their feet that night, until on the morn at nine
> hours not knowing who had win or tint the field.

Quite clearly, by the time night fell on 9 September 1513,
the Earl of Surrey, his commanders and their men knew
that they had won a great victory over their old enemies,
the Scots.

After a battle which had lasted three to four hours, the
English soldiers left on the battlefield must have been
exhausted, and numbed to the scene of slaughter and human
suffering which surrounded them. The surviving Scots, as
they fled across the Tweed, must have been in a state of deep
psychological shock at the terrible outcome of a battle in
which, only a few hours ago, they had seemed to hold all
the advantages. The guilt of surviving such a battle must also
have weighed heavy on their minds. The sun had set on the
scene of Scotland's worst military defeat:

> *For all the lords of their land were left them behind,*
> *beside Brymstone in a brook breathless they lie*
> *gaping against the moon, their ghosts were away.*[77]

5

THE 'FLOWERS OF THE FOREST'

On the morning after the battle, a truly horrific sight must have greeted the English soldiers who stood guard over the captured Scottish ordnance. At the bottom of Branxton Hill, over the space of perhaps one square mile, thousands of human corpses, most of them naked and mutilated, lay thickly on the ground. The small stream, whose unexpected existence had been so disastrous for the Scots, was choked with bodies:

> the streams of blood ran on either side so abundantly that all the fields and waters was made red with the confluence thereof.[1]

The soldiers who were guarding the guns soon had other matters that demanded their attention. A group of perhaps 800 Scots on horseback, almost certainly Lord Home with some of his followers, returned to the battlefield in an attempt to seize the seventeen Scottish guns. The Lord Admiral, with 'a small company', was attacked and a fierce skirmish for possession of the guns ensued. However, William Blackenall, the English Master Gunner 'shot such a peal, that the Scots fled'.[2] Home's last-ditch attempt to save the ordnance had failed, and Lord Dacre made sure that the guns were taken to the safety of Etal Castle and then later to Berwick where they augmented the garrison's artillery. The guns were valued at 1,700 marks, and Bishop Ruthal commented that they were the 'finest that hath been seen'.[3]

With the last spasm of fighting over, the English soldiers began to clean up the appalling carnage of the battlefield, and the little church of Branxton village was used as a temporary mortuary to hold over 1,000 dead.[4] Most of the dead were buried in mass grave pits dug to the south-west of the site of the fiercest fighting. The vast majority of the dead were Scots. English estimates for the total number of Scottish dead ranged from 10,000 to 12,000, but such figures are impossible to substantiate. There would have been no real attempt to count the dead, so the figures given in reports or chronicles are no more than rough estimates. There has always been a tendency to over-inflate the losses of an opponent, but it is generally agreed that ancient and medieval armies always suffered disproportionately high casualties when they were routed or forced to fight at a severe tactical disadvantage. While the figure of 10,000 dead was probably an overenthusiastic English estimate, there seems little reason to question the fact that Scottish losses were heavy and amounted to at least 5,000 and probably as many as 7,000 or 8,000 dead.

The Lord Admiral claimed in the *Articules of Bataille* that English losses amounted to only 400 dead.[5] This figure was inaccurate and was clearly a case of 'talking up' the victory. Hall's chronicle admits to a total figure of 1,500 English casualties in dead, wounded and prisoners. This figure comes from the 'book of wages by which the soldiers were paid'.[6] Yet, from these same accounts, we can learn that while Surrey's personal retinue numbered 500 men at the start of the campaign, only 293 remained alive to be paid off at the end.[7] The fighting at Flodden had been fierce, and although comparatively few English soldiers may have been killed during the battle, there is every reason to suggest that the total number of English casualties may well have been higher than admitted. Bishop Ruthal wrote to Wolsey that:

> few or none being under the same Banner [of St Cuthbert's] were slain, though many hurt.[8]

Many wounded English soldiers who were paid off the strength of the army on 14 September, may well have succumbed to their injuries or secondary infections afterwards. Nonetheless, although English casualties may have been higher than admitted, they were certainly less than the Scots.

It was not simply the number of dead that represented such a body blow to Scotland, but the damage suffered by the first and second 'estates' of Scotland. Sir David Lindsay lamented in his poetic praise of James IV that:

> *I never read in tragedy nor story*
> *At one journay [day] so many nobles slain*
> *For the defence and love of their sovereign.*[9]

It was not until the Great War that once again: 'privileged groups bore a disproportionately heavy burden of war losses'.[10] Yet in 1914–18, the losses fell most heavily upon the young public school boys and undergraduates who made up the majority of the infantry subalterns in the first years of the war.[11] At Flodden, the Scottish nobility and gentry as a class, along with many clergy, had suffered terrible losses. Packed into the front ranks of the Scottish pike columns, these men had neither wished, nor been able, to flee. With the ferocity of the fighting, and the unwillingness to take prisoners, virtually an entire generation of Scottish noblemen and gentry had been wiped out in a single afternoon. Alexander Stewart, the king's bastard son who held the positions of Chancellor of Scotland and Archbishop of St Andrews, had been killed along with George Hepburn, the Bishop of the Isles, two abbots and the Dean of Glasgow Cathedral. Nine earls out of a total of twenty-one had been killed, and fourteen lords of Parliament out of twenty-nine had also died on the field.[12] The battle also cut a swathe through the knights, gentry and lairds of Scotland, who suffered at least 300 casualties.[13] Yet strangely enough, no family line died out due to the deaths at Flodden. Often the father, the head of a household, was killed alongside his older sons, leaving only the youngest son to carry on the family name and responsibilities. In one example of many, David Pringle of Smailholm, laird of Galashiels, was killed along with his four sons. His fifth son, still a child, became the new laird. The cities and burghs of Scotland also suffered heavily. The Provost of Edinburgh was killed alongside many of his burgesses and those of Glasgow, Perth and Aberdeen. Indeed, it is easier to determine which of the Scottish nobles survived the battle than to provide an exact list of all those who died. Out of the higher ranks of nobles who fought at Flodden, only the Earl of Huntly, Lord Home and Lord Lindsay survived the battle. We also know that

Archibald Napier, laird of Merchiston, Sir Andrew Kerr of Ferniehurst and Iain Mackenzie, clan chief of the Mackenzies, survived the battle. Iain Mackenzie had the dubious distinction to live long enough to witness another Scottish defeat at the battle of Pinkie in 1547. Only Sir John Forman, Sir William Scott of Balwearie, Sir John Colquhoun and James Logan were important enough to be mentioned as individual prisoners in English accounts.[14] The loss of almost an entire generation of the ruling and administrative classes was a terrible blow for a feudal society. The noblemen who had understood and accepted James IV's powerful monarchy, and demonstrated their loyalty to his kingship through personal service on the battlefield, were almost all dead. These heavy losses amongst Scotland's political élite left a considerable political vacuum. The promise and reality of James IV's powerful and popular rule of Scotland had been snuffed out. Erasmus, the great humanist scholar of the age, who had tutored the brilliant young Alexander Stewart, lamented Stewart's death:

> What hadst thou to do with fierce Mars... thou that wert destined for the Muses and for Christ?[15]

However, the greatest loss suffered by Scotland was the death of her king, James IV. The 'rose nobill' of Scotland had been gambled, risked and lost. Although the English commanders knew that James had fallen, his body was not found until the next day. James's body was covered with:

> diverse deadly wounds and in especial one with an arrow, and another with a bill as appeared when he was naked.[16]

Lord Dacre, who had been a guest at James's wedding and had hawked and played cards with the king during an Anglo-Scottish raid on the lawless borders in 1504, recognised the king's body and brought it off the field.[17]

The body was taken to Berwick where it was shown to Sir William Scott, the king's sergeant porter, and his counsellor Sir John Forman, 'which knew him at the first sight and made great lamentation'.[18] The body was embalmed and placed in a lead coffin. It was then secretly transported to Newcastle 'amongst other stuff'[19] and then to London. Bishop Ruthal had tried to persuade Sir Phillip Tylney to leave the body at Durham, but he had to be satisfied with the king of Scots' Standard, and the 'harness for his thighs' as trophies for St Cuthbert's Church.[20] Meanwhile, a piece of James's bloodied and torn surcoat was sent enthusiastically by Queen Katherine to Henry VIII in France.

James's body was eventually transported to the Carthusian monastery of Sheen, near Richmond, where it lay while Henry dealt with the difficult question of how to treat the body of the excommunicated king of Scots. By breaking the 'Treaty of Perpetual Peace', James had automatically drawn the penalty of excommunication upon himself and this meant that his body could not be buried in sanctified ground. However, the pope wrote to Henry asking him to give James a state funeral in St Paul's Cathedral. Before burial, the Bishop of London was asked to perform the penitential rites giving absolution from the sentence of excommunication.[21] Unfortunately, Henry VIII seems to have lost interest in the matter and the body of his brother-in-law, the king of Scots, lay unburied at Richmond for many years.

After the dissolution of the monasteries, the body was left in a lumber room amongst rubbish. John Stow tells a gruesome story that:

> workmen there for their foolish pleasure, hewed off his head; and Lancelot Young, master glazier to Queen Elizabeth, feeling a sweet savour to come from thence, and seeing this same dried from all moisture, and yet the form remaining, with the hair of the head and beard red, brought it to London, to his house in Wood Street, where for a time he kept it for its sweetness, but in the end caused the sexton of that church [St Michael's], to bury it amongst other bones taken out of their charnel.[22]

By the time that James VI took the throne of England, his great-grandfather's bones had long been lost in anonymity. The last resting places of a brave and determined king of Scots remain to this day unmarked and undignified.

When the English commanders returned to their camp at Barmoor, they discovered that some of the Borderers who had fled at the noise of the Scottish artillery had plundered the camp:

> Many men lost their horses, and such stuff as they left in their tents and pavilions, by the robbers of Tynedale and Tweeddale.[23]

This must have been very disheartening to soldiers who had just fought a hard battle. Ruthal commented that:

> our folks were worse discouraged at their departing thence, than by all the harm done to them by the Scots.[24]

On 14 September, five days after the battle, the Earl of Surrey promptly disbanded his army. He proudly stated that he had managed to save the wages of 18,689 men for a fortnight by adopting this 'policy'.[25] His men, replete with their plunder from the battlefield, were probably happy enough to go home although 'many a wee [man] wanted his horse and wandered home on foot'[26] due to the depredations of the Borderers. While the English soldiers cursed the Borderers when they saw their plundered camp at Barmoor, and grumbled at losing out on two weeks pay as they marched home, their situation was infinitely better than the Scottish survivors of the battle. Polydore Vergil tells us that:

> On the following night, the Scottish army, ravaging as it went, returned homewards; and, when it reached Scotland, it heard on all sides the unwelcome words, that it had been unreasonable and unpatriotic of them, neither to have avenged the death of the King, nor to have seen to the succour of their perishing countrymen; and that thus their country was branded with everlasting disgrace.[27]

If 8,000 Scots were killed during the fight, perhaps as many as 20,000 survived the battle. The guilt of surviving such a battle must have weighed heavy on these men who, totally lacking supplies which had all been abandoned in their well-appointed camp, had to plunder and raid their own countrymen to survive. While the Scottish population heaped scorn and spite on the survivors of the army, those survivors in their turn blamed the French advisors:

> Of the Frenchmen who served in the Scottish army, some fell in the engagement, others were cut to pieces by the

Scots, who reproached the French with being the cause of their destruction.[28]

It was a sad end to one of the largest French military missions ever sent to Scotland.

News of Flodden had already reached Edinburgh by 10 September, although the reports remained unconfirmed rumours which were not accepted by the burgh council. The council sternly ordered that:

All women, and especially vagabonds… be not seen upon the street clamouring and crying, under the pain of banishing of their persons without favour, and the other women of better sort pass to the Kirk and pray, when time requires, for our Sovereign Lord and his army, and the townsmen who are with the army.[29]

When the rumours were confirmed, and the reality of the disaster dawned on the Scottish capital, the grief amongst its population can only have been redoubled. Fearing a devastating English invasion, the burgh council decided to build a wall around the unprotected portion of the city. This wall was hastily thrown up to defend the Scottish capital but remained untested by English assault.[30]

When the news of Flodden reached Henry in France on 25 September, he ordered all his cannon fired in celebration:

The King of Scots is killed, with all his cursed lords'. When the King, of his kindness, heard these words, he said, 'I will sing him a soul knell with the sound of my guns.' Such a noise, to my name, was never heard before, for there was shot at a shot a thousand at once, that all rang with the Rowte, Rocher and other.[31]

The city of Tournai, chastened by the fate of Thérouanne, had surrendered the day before after a siege of just eight days. A solemn *Te Deum* was sung in the newly captured cathedral of Tournai to give thanks for the victory over the Scots. Although Henry had given Thérouanne to Maximilian, he kept Tournai as a prize and, after three weeks of feasting, Henry returned to England. His progress across the Channel was unhindered by the combined Franco-Scottish fleet which had been unable to turn its formidable threat into a reality.

Indeed, the powerful Scottish fleet which had sailed with confidence in July 1513 ended the campaign disheartened and depleted. A series of storms dispersed the combined Franco-Scottish fleet after it had finally assembled in Normandy in September 1513. The *Michael*, pride of the Scottish fleet, ran aground and could not be refloated. Eventually, she was sold to Louis XII for £18,000 Scots on 2 April 1514, after only two and a half years in Scottish service.[32] The Scottish soldiers who returned home from the fleet even complained of mistreatment by their French hosts.

It is said that the young Queen Margaret waited for the return of her husband in a tower at Linlithgow Palace. While the people of Scotland were undoubtedly grief-stricken at the losses of the fathers, husbands and sons they had suffered, the government of Scotland was not paralysed even with the loss of so many nobles and officials. In the immediate aftermath of the disaster, the government of Scotland remained remarkably resilient. Only ten days after Flodden, the lords of council met at Stirling to reorganise the government of Scotland. The new membership of the daily council was agreed upon, arrangements for the coronation of James V were put in hand, and a general council of all the magnates was called to organise the defence of Scotland. As an emergency measure, Lord Home was given responsibility for law and order on the borders, the Earl of Argyll was given control over the west and the Earl of Huntly the north. Margaret's son James was just seventeen months old, but he was crowned King James V of Scots on 21 September 1513 in the Chapel Royal at Stirling Castle.[33]

As the daily council worked feverishly to reorganise the administration and to appoint new sheriffs and judges, the general council met on 26 November 1513 at Perth and decided to invite John, Duke of Albany, to return from France and accept the position of Governor of Scotland during the king's minority. The alliance with France was confirmed. Even though Scotland had suffered a heavy defeat at Flodden, the council saw no reason to abandon the policy of war with England. Indeed, now the lords of Scotland were determined to avenge the terrible reverse they had suffered. Lord Fleming was sent as the Scottish representative to France before the end of 1513 to continue planning Franco-Scottish co-operation against England. Orders were sent that important castles were to be garrisoned and *wapinschaws* were to be held throughout the country to guard against an English invasion. The council of Scotland also appointed Margaret as *tutrix* to the young king, in accordance with James IV's will.[34]

Thus, although Scotland remained in shock after the events of Flodden, her government worked quickly to regain much needed stability. Unfortunately, although much hard work was done by such stalwarts as William Elphinstone (Bishop of Aberdeen, Keeper of the Privy Seal), James Beaton, Archbishop of Glasgow (now Chancellor of Scotland), and Patrick Paniter, the king's secretary who had survived Flodden and now worked once again on royal correspondence, rifts between members of the council began appearing as early as January 1514. Wrangles over who should fill the vacant sees of St Andrews, the Isles, Kilwinning and Inchaffray, disputes between the queen and the daily council, and divisions within the council of Scotland over foreign policy all became intractable problems during the spring of 1514.[35]

The summer of 1514 brought renewed crisis to Scotland. Henry VIII had made earnest preparations in late 1513 to resume his campaign in France the next year, but his plans for further military adventures came to nothing. The 'Holy League' fell apart in March 1514 and an Anglo–French truce was signed that month. In a rapid *volte face* of policy engineered by Cardinal Wolsey, Henry signed a peace treaty with France on 7 August 1514 and gave his youngest sister Mary as bride to the aged Louis XII of France. Even after the accession of a new French king, Francis I, in 1515, the French continued the policy of rapprochement with England. With the French now courting the support of the English king, French support for Scotland, which had been bought at such a high price, evaporated.[36] What was worse was that the Peace Treaty agreed between England and France was insulting to the Scots. The Treaty included Scotland, even though the document was signed without the knowledge or consent of the council of Scotland. There was also a clause which prohibited Scottish raids against England, but which remained silent about any English raids against Scotland. It is inconceivable that, if James IV had returned victorious from his campaign in Northumberland, the king of Scots would not have been included in the negotiations for peace. Indeed, it was precisely due to this desire to have a strong negotiating position at the conclusion of a peace treaty, that James had gone to war in the first place. Although Henry refused to invade Scotland in the immediate aftermath of Flodden, claiming that it was not seemly to make war on a widow and child, he ensured that he remained well informed on Scottish affairs and continued to interfere with the affairs of Scotland for the rest of his reign. While James IV had pursued an independent policy for Scotland, his death led to both France and England attempting to manipulate the affairs of a weakened Scotland.

On 6 August 1514, the day before France and England made peace, Queen Margaret astonished the lords of Scotland by marrying her second husband, the Earl of Angus, the grandson of 'Bell-the-Cat'. By marrying into the Douglas faction, Margaret had unwittingly opened old wounds and quarrels between rival groups of Scottish lords. The council revoked her right to act as *tutrix* to the young king and her challenge to the council's decision, supported by the Douglas faction, led to violence.[37] Scotland descended into the instability of intermittent factional violence and political in-fighting which had always blighted the minority of a king of Scots.

Henry remained ambivalent (not to say embarrassed) about the stunning victory at Flodden, probably because it so outshone his own military achievements in France. While his 'victory' at the 'Battle of the Spurs' was immortalised by court painters and in story and song, there was no such official royal treatment of Flodden. That battle against the 'auld enemy' remained a relatively unheralded victory remembered mainly in the north of England. Although Surrey knighted a number of English gentry on the field, he had to wait rather longer for his own reward. In 1514, Henry restored his family's ducal title, which had been lost at Bosworth.[38] The Howards were Dukes of Norfolk once again. His son Thomas, the Lord Admiral, gained his father's title of the Earl of Surrey, while Sir Edward Stanley was made Lord Monteagle in memory of his Stanley retainers who had climbed the 'mont' of Branxton Hill.[39] Although Surrey, the Lord Admiral, Stanley, and other English captains received letters of royal thanks, none of them received the financial rewards that they might have expected had their exploits been under the king's eye. Almost all of the English commanders felt that their monarch did not fully recognise their contribution to the only real victory of the 1513 campaign.[40]

Henry's campaign in France had exhausted his treasury but achieved very little. Indeed, the cost of his military adventures had been cripplingly high. From his accession until 12 June 1513, the Treasurer of the Chamber, the main finance officer of the crown, had disbursed just over £1 million, with the vast majority paid out on military expeditions.[41] Henry had not achieved imperishable military glory, and the capture of the two towns of Thérouanne and Tournai as the sole achievement of an army of 30,000 men was faintly pathetic, given the enormous cost involved. Even though Cardinal Bainbridge pressed the pope to come and crown Henry the new king of France at Rheims, Pope Leo X

The Heraldic Augmentation of the 'Royal Shield of Scotland', having a demi-lion only, pierced through the mouth with an arrow, granted by Henry VIII to Thomas Howard, Earl of Surrey, in commemoration of his victory at Flodden; borne on the family arms for posterity.

wisely distanced himself from his predecessor's extravagant promises.[42]

An English tinker called John Brown was recorded as having discussed the recent battle in the house of Thomas Graynger, the pewterer in Hereford, on 20 April 1514. Graynger informed the Mayor of Hereford that Brown had:

> talked of the Scottish field, and said though the Scots lost their King they lost no field... he said that he had seen and knew the King of Scots ordnance, which were as goodly ordnances as any was in the world, and though they were lost they would have as good again. Also he said that the Scots would come again into England unto Hamstone [meaning, Branxton].[43]

In fact, the evil memory of Flodden hung over Scottish military expeditions for decades. In July 1522, the Duke of

Albany organised a large force to invade England in co-operation with Francis I, who had reversed his policy of friendship with England. However, this time the Scots would not attack England in support of a French policy. Albany's seemingly impressive army melted away. In 1523, the Scottish Parliament decided on war. Yet when the Scots – again under Albany's command – reached the Tweed, most of the troops refused to cross the river that had marked James IV's Rubicon. Albany besieged Wark Castle with a force mainly composed of French troops, but had to abandon the siege when Thomas Howard, the Lord Admiral at Flodden and now the Duke of Norfolk, approached with a relief force.[44] The strengthened defences of the rebuilt Norham Castle were not even put to the test. When the adult James V organised an army to attack England in 1542, many nobles absented themselves, and even those who marched to war showed a marked reluctance to cross the border. The large Scottish force was crossing the wide estuary of the Solway Firth, when a small force of English Border 'prickers' mounted a series of small spoiling attacks. The Scottish force dissolved in panic and suffered heavy casualties in a humiliating disaster.[45] Flodden cast a long shadow over Scottish affairs.

The shock and trauma of the bloody events of Flodden caused many Scots to disbelieve and deny the reality of what had happened to their king and army. James had committed himself to a strategy which encompassed great personal risk, but more importantly, enormous risk for Scotland. Later Scottish chroniclers, and indeed the people of Scotland, found it difficult to accept that their popular and strong king had hazarded everything on the battlefield and lost.

Life in Scotland after Flodden with its political turmoil, violence and instability seemed to contrast sharply with the 'aureate age' of James IV's reign, when Scotland was prosperous, respected and independent. Very soon after the battle, rumours and tales concerning the fateful campaign of 1513 began to grow in Scotland. One of the most persistent rumours was that the king had somehow survived the battle. Queen Margaret even claimed to the pope, in her petition of divorce from the Earl of Angus, that she had married Angus in error because at the time of her second marriage there were reports that her first husband, James IV, was still alive.[46] Pitscottie filled his famous account of the campaign of 1513 with portents of doom. The 'man clad in a blue gown' who appeared before the king at Linlithgow, the 'summons of Pluto' and even the supposed 'adultery' with Lady Ford were all signs which James should have recognised and thus averted his country's doom.[47] Pitscottie also tells of four mysterious horsemen who:

> rode in the field and horsed the King and brought him forth of the field on a dun hackney. But some says they had him in the Merse betwixt Duns and Kelso. What they did with him there I can not tell.[48]

There were also many rumours that the English had not identified James's body but had taken a dead Scots noble dressed in James's 'coat armour'.[49] Most of the stories suggested that James was still living, but had gone on pilgrimage to Jerusalem to pay penance for his sins. Even if James IV had survived the battle, the storytellers agreed that he was lost to Scotland, 'however the matter come, he appeared not in Scotland after as King'.[50] All of the tales grew out of the need within the Scottish people to understand the calamity that had befallen them.

While the Scots felt that there had to be some kind of explanation for the disaster at Flodden which haunted their folk memory, no such explanation was necessary for the English. English armies had invariably defeated the Scots in battle, and Roger Ascham's proud boast that 'Every English archer beareth under his girdle twenty four Scots'[51] was still taken on trust, even though the longbow had failed at Flodden. With Henry VIII's ambivalent attitude to the victory, it was left to the north of England, and the communities who had sent men to the battle, to commemorate their achievements. Leigh of Baggerley's ballad *Scotish Feilde* was written as praise for the Stanley family and their achievements at Flodden, as well as providing some sort of explanation for the rout of the Lancashire and Cheshire men under Edmund Howard. Another poem, *Flodden Feilde* was also written under Stanley patronage, but concerned itself more with past events and the campaign in France than with the battle itself.[52] While the Scots did not want to be reminded of their defeat, some English knights and their communities did erect memorials and monuments to their soldiers. Sir Richard Assheton paid for a stained glass window in his local church of St Leonard's in his town of Middleton that remains one of the earliest war memorials in Britain. The window illustrated Sir Richard and his wife, along with the archers of Middleton that he had taken to the battle. St Oswald's Church at Arncliffe, in the Yorkshire Dales, also contains a list of the men of Littondale, Arncliffe and Hawswick, who fought at the battle. Sir Marmaduke

Here lieth Marmaduke Cunstable of Flaynborght Knyght
Who made aduento into France for the right of the same
Passed ouer with Kyng Edwarde the Fouriht yᵗ noble Knight
And also with noble king herre the seuinth of that name
He was also at Barwik at the winnyng of the same
And by Kyg Edward chosy Captey there first of any one
And rewllid & gouernid ther his tyme without blame
But for all that as ye se he lieth vnder this stone

At brankisto feld wher the Kyng of Scottys was slayne
He then beyng of the age of thre score and tene
With the gode Duke uf northefolke yᵗ iorney he hay tayn
And coragely abancid hyself emog other there & then
The Kig beyng i France with gret nombre of yglesh me
He nothyng hedyng his age ther but jeopde hy as on
With his sonnes brothe saruantt and kynnismen
But now as ye se he lyeth under this stone

Extract from the text of the brass memorial to Sir Marmaduke Constable,
Flamborough, Yorkshire.

Constable's memorial brass commemorates the venerable soldier's exploits in France and at Flodden, although it wisely omits to mention his service under Richard III.

The sting of the disaster at Flodden faded over the years, but the memory of the shock and grief remained within Scottish folk tradition. In the eighteenth century, Jane Walter Elliot heard an old Scots folk tune, which moved her to write a new poem called *A Lament for Flodden*.[53] The haunting tune and moving lyrics *The Flowers of the Forest* continue to inspire singers and songwriters. Sir Walter Scott, that most enthusiastic of all Scottish historians and antiquarians of the nineteenth century, did much to reawaken interest in the battle but also overlaid Victorian ideals of chivalry and knightly conduct onto the story. In Scott's epic poem *Marmion*, the story of star-crossed love reaches its climax on the field of Flodden. In Scott's powerful poem, 'charging knights like whirlwinds go', while the Scots stood grimly around their dead king:

> *Unbroken was the ring;*
> *The stubborn spear-men still made good*
> *Their dark impenetrable wood*
> *Each stepping where his comrade stood,*
> *The instant that he fell.*[54]

Scott's language is heady and evocative but it can also be misleading. In *Tales of a Grandfather*, Scott's history of Scotland, James IV is criticised for his chivalrous notions. This is a re-direction of Pitscottie's 'sensual pleasures' into a more acceptable format but, unfortunately, this view of James as a romantic, chivalrous fool has persisted to the present day. Scott's *Marmion* inspired many artists, composers and playwrights. Ayton's *Edinburgh After Flodden* was another poetic *tour de force* that was very popular during the nineteenth century.[55] Albert Sullivan, more famous for his musical scores in the Gilbert and Sullivan comic operas, composed a symphony named *Marmion* which was well received at the time.

However, it is only in the borders of Scotland that the memory of Flodden is formally commemorated today. Selkirk tradition maintains that, out of the eighty who had gone on campaign, only one man, named Fletcher, returned to the town from the battle, carrying an English standard which he held aloft and then cast on the ground. This banner, which still exists, was carried by the Macclesfield contingent led by Sir Christopher Savage. This legend came to be associated with the annual ritual known as the 'Common Riding', where riders carrying flags representing the trades and corporations of the town ride around the boundaries of the burgh. The ceremony is complete when all of the colours are cast to the ground in the market place.[56]

Most of the literature, histories, stories and songs which surround the campaign of 1513 draw their inspiration from the dramatic defeat suffered by the Scots. Even today it can be difficult to understand why the Scots suffered such a disaster at the bottom of Branxton Hill. The military campaign waged by the Scots prior to the afternoon of 9 September 1513 had been an outstanding success. James IV had attempted to preserve peace, and his beneficial state of neutrality, for as long as possible, but when this was no longer a realistic diplomatic option, he had attempted to gain the best price for his military intervention in a wider European war. Scottish preparations for war, even while attempting to maintain peace, were thorough, efficient and well-planned. James IV even managed to gain a high degree of unanimity amongst his nobles and broad popular support for his war with England. The campaign waged by the Scots in Northumberland was short but sharp. Norham Castle, the main objective, fell within six days and left the English border open and vulnerable. The Scots' position on Flodden Edge was well chosen and presented the Earl of Surrey with considerable difficulties and a real dilemma. Even after the impressive English flank march, the Scots army still managed to maintain the psychological advantage through its careful deployment on Branxton Hill and the 'crafty' use of a smokescreen. As late as 4 p.m. on 9 September 1513, the Scots were confident of success and seemed to hold all the advantages of ground, numbers and weaponry in the coming engagement. It is certainly true, as von Moltke remarked, that 'no plan survives the first contact with the enemy', but nothing could have prepared the Scots for the disastrous consequences of the battle.

Many, many explanations have been advanced to explain the defeat suffered by the Scots. These began as early as 16 January 1514, when a letter from the very young James V, written by his council, was sent to King Hans of Denmark. It was claimed that the late king of Scots had been impatient at the sight of them (the English) and, 'keeping no order among his men', many of whom were 'peasants and inexperienced in military service', had rushed from his strong position to attack the enemy.[57]

This remarkably sensible and balanced explanation was soon joined by Pitscottie's colourful stories of portents of doom, 'whoredom and harlotry' and wilful dismissal of wise counsel. Pitscottie believed the disaster had occurred because James had not recognised these signs, but more importantly had refused to accept the wise council of his lords and councillors. The battle of Flodden was lost, according to Pitscottie, not because of:

> the manhood nor wisdom of Englishmen but by the King's own wilful misgovernance that would use no counsel of his wise nobles and aged lords.

James had indulged in 'his own sensual pleasures which was the cause of his ruin'. For Pitscottie, James IV was an example to all princes that they should accept 'honest and goodly counsel'.[58] The addition by Sir Walter Scott of fanciful suggestions of romance, chivalry and hot-headedness did nothing to advance the real causes for the Scottish defeat.[59]

The fact was that James IV, his nobles and his French military advisors, had not made any serious errors of military judgement before the battle began. However, the ensuing combat cruelly exposed the hidden flaws and frailties in the Scottish military machine. The very impressive Scottish guns failed to perform to the high expectations of them. The 'seven sisters' and their cousins were highly effective pieces of siege artillery, but were not capable of effective use in battle. James IV's decision to mount an all-out attack when his artillery failed was far from mistaken. The Scottish pike columns posed a very real threat to the English army, as was revealed by Home and Huntly's rout of Edmund Howard's battle. Unfortunately, the existence of a small, marshy stream at the bottom of Branxton Hill, which lay unnoticed while the Scots were at the top of the hill, brought disaster as it broke up the close formation of the two other Scottish pike columns. When the pike failed, the Scots had no viable alternative, and, under the pressure of a desperately close fight, the morale of the ordinary Scottish soldier, illtrained and unprepared for the situation, broke. The Scots had invested heavily in the new military technology but had failed to make a similar investment – because of its cost and complexity – in the important subtleties of supporting weapons such as halberds, crossbows, two-handed swords or the veterans who wielded them in continental battles. If even a small proportion of the Scots soldiers within the pike columns had been armed with the Swiss halberd or the *dopplensolder's* two-handed sword, the fight with the English billmen would not have been so one-sided. Most importantly of all, the Scots had not spent sufficient time on the intangible but vital element of training. In the critical test of battle, it was the lack of discipline, knowledge of drill and cohesion which could only be fostered by hard training, that brought disaster to the Scots at the bottom of Branxton Hill. The reliance on the Scottish tradition of the feudal nobility and gentry leading from the front to stiffen the mass of soldiers could not compensate for the lack of training, or the tactical brittleness of the Scots military machine and simply led to the slaughter of those elites on the battlefield.

However, while the Scots struggled to find an explanation for the disaster within themselves, this could only ever be half of the story. The strengths and capabilities of the English army which inflicted such damage on the Scots have often been overlooked. There is no doubt that the Earl of Surrey and his subordinate commanders were experienced and capable. Similarly, the English system of raising troops meant that many of the English soldiers were well trained in the use of their weapons, even if they did not have experience of battle. This made a tremendous difference to the capabilities of the English army which marched and fought with consistent ability. The long flank march mounted by Surrey and the hasty re-organisation of his battles just before combat were only possible because the English officers and men knew their trade. The English army was also not let down by its tactical system which, even if outdated, still functioned effectively. The light English artillery was well suited to field use and was capable of suppressing its Scottish opponents. The combination of archers and billmen had evolved during the fourteenth and fifteenth centuries and had been a remarkably effective system which could cope with most opponents and tactical situations. The bloody and interminable battles of the Wars of the Roses had simply honed English forces to a fine edge. Surrey's army was able to exploit the hidden weaknesses present in the Scottish force.

Yet Flodden was the last battle in the British Isles when the old English military system functioned effectively. Flodden had proved that the longbow was now an obsolete weapon against well-armoured troops. Although the English were emotionally attached to the weapon, the longbow was gradually replaced by the arquebus and musket in English armies. By 1547, when the English fought the Scots at the battle of Pinkie, the English army had been transformed from the bill and bow combination into a balanced force of cavalry, infantry and artillery. The Scots, still reliant on the pike and still deficient in artillery, supporting arms and training, went down to defeat in the last battle between Scotland and England as independent countries.[60]

James IV's death on the battlefield did not spare him from criticism. Polydore Vergil remarked that:

> such an end to his life James was forced to suffer, that he might atone by his death for his violation of the Treaty.[61]

Hall wrote of him:

> O what a noble and triumphant courage was this for a king to fight in a battle as a mean soldier. But what availed his

strong harness, the puissance of his mighty champions with whom he descended the hill, in whom he so much trusted that with his strong people and great number of men, he was able, as he thought, to have vanquished that day the greatest prince of the world, if he had been there as the Earl of Surrey was, or else he thought to do such a high enterprise himself in his person, that should surmount the enterprises of all other princes, but however it happened God gave the stroke, and he was no more regarded than a poor soldier, for all went one way. This may be a great mirror to all Princes, how that they adventure themselves in such a battle.[62]

Victory might be won on the battlefield, but the risks and price of glory were too high for kings to 'adventure themselves' in battle as James had done. In contrast, Henry VIII had been kept safe during his campaign in France. Surrounded by his bodyguard of picked and loyal nobles, the English king had been kept deliberately out of the way of any real danger.[63] Bishop Ruthal had noted that:

in the conserving of his noble person dependeth the weal and surety of his realm and all the nobles and others of his army, whereas of the contrary (which God defend!) the loss and destruction of all may follow.[64]

The English had been well-aware of the enormous cost they would have to pay if their sovereign was killed on campaign.

However, King James IV of Scotland has perhaps received more criticism for his conduct of the campaign of 1513 and the battle of Flodden than he deserved. James had hoped to win status and prestige amongst the monarchs of Europe for Scotland's involvement in a European war, while also reminding his arrogant brother-in-law, Henry VIII, of the power of an independent Scotland. Instead, James paid the ultimate personal price for leading his men in battle and Scotland suffered disaster with the loss of her king, nobles and army in one afternoon. However, perhaps the hidden tragedy of 1513 for Scotland was that the Scots' campaign, shrewdly financed mainly by France, well prepared militarily, soundly planned, organised and fought for limited and achievable objectives, came to such bitter grief. It was Henry VIII who had impossible dreams of conquest, who had spent a fortune on a strategically insignificant campaign in France, and who was manipulated and used by his erstwhile allies, Pope Julius II, Ferdinand of Aragon and the Emperor Maximillian. But Henry, who had precipitated the war between Scotland and England, came out of the war of 1513 with his person and kingdom intact save for the enormous expense of his wrong-headed and vainglorious schemes. James IV paid for his defeat in battle with his life. It is doubly ironic then, that for so long the Scots have accorded the sins of Henry VIII to their much more hard-headed but unfortunate ruler, James IV.

MAPS

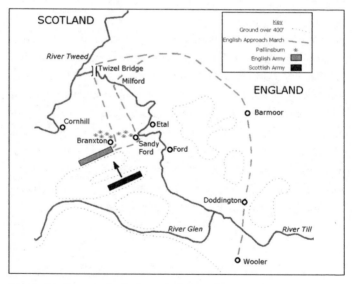

Map 1 This illustrates the flank march of the English army and the original deployment of the Scots army on Flodden Edge.

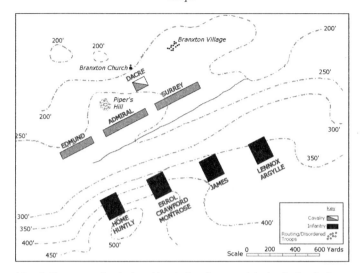

Map 2 The two armies deployed just before the start of the battle. Stanley's men are still marching up to the battlefield.

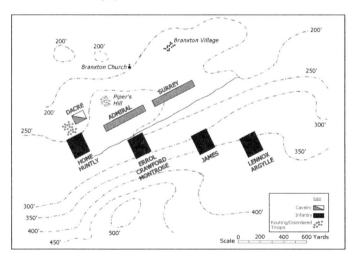

Map 3 The Scottish columns mount an *echelon* attack on the English line. Howard's battle has dissolved in rout and Dacre's horsemen have come up to restore the situation on the English right flank.

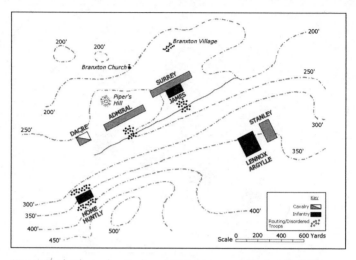

Map 4 The battle reaches its climax. While Home and Huntly rally their men, the king's battle, along with Erroll, Crawford and Montrose's column, has disintegrated. Stanley's men, having climbed Branxton Hill, attack Lennox and Argyll.

APPENDIX I

List of the Principal Dead at Flodden

SCOTTISH LOSSES

King James IV of Scotland
Alexander Stewart, Archbishop of St Andrews, Chancellor of Scotland
George Hepburn, Bishop of the Isles
Lawrence Oliphant, Abbott of Inchaffray
William Bunch, Abbott of Kilwinning

Earls (9 killed)

Earl of Argyll	Earl of Bothwell
Earl of Caithness	Earl of Cassillis
Earl of Crawford	Earl of Erroll
Earl of Lennox	Earl of Rothes
Earl of Montrose	

The Earl of Huntly survived the battle.

Lords of Parliament (14 killed)

Avondale	Crichton
Elphinstone	Erskine
Hay of Yester	Herries
Keith	Lorne
Maxwell	Oliphant
Ross	Sempill
Seton	Sinclair

Darnley, the son of Lord Lennox
Lord Home and Lord Patrick Lindsay of the Byres survived the battle.

Survivors

Sir Andrew Kerr of Ferniehurst
Alexander McNaughten
Patrick Paniter, the king's secretary
Robert Borthwick, the king's Master Meltar and Gunner

Prisoners

Sir John Forman
Sir William Scot of Balwearie
John Skirving of Plewlandhill
James Logan

ENGLISH LOSSES

Sir Brian Tunstall
Sir William Fitzwilliam
Sir Richard Harbottle
Sir Ralph Warcoppe
Sir Christopher Savage
Sir William Handforth
Sir John Booth
Sir John Gower
Robert Fouleshurst
Maurice Berkeley
John Sankey
John Bostock
Thomas Venables

Prisoners

Sir Humphrey Lisle
Mr Henry Gray

Note: These lists of losses at Flodden cannot be considered exhaustive. They are, however, compiled from the best estimates and information available.

APPENDIX II

The Strength of the English and Scottish Armies at Flodden

Scotland		England	
Home and Huntly	8,000	Edmund Howard	3,000
Erroll, Crawford			
& Montrose	6,000	Lord Admiral	9,000
King James IV	9,000	Surrey	5,000
Lennox and Argyll	6,000	Edward Stanley	4,000
		Lord Dacre	1,500
Totals	29,000		22,500

These figures are strictly estimates and represent the likely strengths of the units of the opposing armies after the English reorganisation which took place just before the battle. They are based on the figures contained in the contemporary sources and the figures contained in J.D. Mackie, 'The English Army at Flodden', *Miscellany of the Scottish History Society*, vol. VIII, Edinburgh, 1951, and Fitzwilliam Andrew Elliot, *The Battle of Flodden and the Raids of 1513*, Edinburgh, 1911.

APPENDIX III

Articules of the Bataille bitwix the Kynge of Scottes and therle of Surrey in Brankstone felde the 9 day of Septembre

Furst, whenne bothe tharmyes were within three myles togidres, the said Erle sent Rugecrosse to the Kynge of Scottes desiryng hym of bataille, and he answered he wolde abyde hym there tylle Fryday at none.

The Lorde Hawarde at 11 of the cloke the said nine day, passed over the brigge of Twysselle with the vawarde and artyllary, and the said Erle folawynge with the rerewarde, tharmy was devyded in to two batalles, and to eithre bataille two wynges.

The Kynge of Scottes army was devided into five batailles, and every bataille an arrowe shotte from the other, and alle like ferns from the Englisshe armye in grete plumpes, parte of them quadrant, and somme pyke wyse, and were on the toppe of the hylle, being a quarter of a myle from the fote therof.

The Lord Hawarde caused his vawarde to stale in a lytelle valley tylle the rerewarde were joined to oon of the wynges of his bataille, and then both wardes in oon fronte avaunced against the Scottes, and they cam downe the hille and mette with them in good ordre after the Almayns maner withoute spekying of eny worde.

Therles of Huntley, Arell, and Crawford, with theire host of 6,000 men, cam upon the Lord Hawarde, and shortly theire bakkes were tourned, and the most parte of theym slayne.

The Kynge of Scottes cam with a grete puyssaunce upon my Lorde of Surrey, having on his lyfte hande my Lorde Darcy son, whiche two bare alle the brounte of the bataille, and there the Kynge of Scottes was slayne within a spere lengthe from the said Erle of Surrey, and many noble men of the Scottes slayn moo, and no prisoners taken in thees two batailles. And in the tyme of this bataille therles of Lynewes and Argylle, with theire pusaunces, joined with Sir Edwarde Stanley, and they were putte to flyghte. Edmonde Howarde hadde with hym 1,000 Cheshire men and 500 Lancashire men and many gentilmen of Yorkshire on the righte wynge of the Lorde Hawarde, and the Lorde Chamberlain of Scotlande with many lordes dyd sette on hym and the Chesshire and Lancasshire men never abode stroke, and fewe of the gentilmen of Yorkshire abode but fled, Master Gray and Sir Humpfrey Lyle be taken prisoners, and Sir Wynchard Hartbotelle amd Maurys Barkeley slayne, and the saide Edmonde Hawarde was thries feled, and to his relief the Lord Dacres cam with 1,500 men, and put to flighte alle the said Scottes, and had about 8 score of his men slayne. In whiche bataille a grete nombre of Scottes were slayne.

The bataille and conflytte beganne bitwixt four and five at after none, and the chace con-
tynued three myles with mervelous slawter, and 10,000 moo had been slayn if the
Englisshemen had be on horsbak.

The Scottes were 80,000 and about 10,000 of them slayn and under 400 Englisshemen
slayn.

~~The borders not only stale away as they left 4 or 5000 horses, but also they toke away the~~
~~oxen that drewe thordynaunce, and cam to the pavilyons and toke away alle the stuffe therin,~~
~~and kylled many that kept the same.~~

Thenglisshe and Scottisshe ordinaunce is conveyed by the goode helpe of the Lorde Dacre
unto Etalle Castelle.

The King of Scottes body is brought to Berwycke, ther is noo grete man of Scotlande
retorned home but the Chamberlain. It is thought that fewe of them bee lefte on lyve.

Hic finis

The Lorde Howarde Admyralle purposet to &c.

Henry James (ed.), 'Account of the Battle of Flodden, Articules of the Bataille bitwix
the Kynge of Scottes and therle of Surrey in Brankstone felde the 9 day of Septembre',
in Henry James (ed.), *Facsimiles of National Manuscripts from William the Conqueror to
Queen Anne*, Southampton, 1865, pp.2-3.

APPENDIX IV

Extract from *The Trewe Encountre*

*Immediately, my Lorde Hawarde with the vawarde, and my Lord of Surrey with the rere-
warde in thair mooste qwyke and spedy maner avaunced and made towarde the said King
of Scots as faste as to thaim was possible in array, and what for the hilles and smoke long
it was or the array of the Scotts couth be conceived, and at the laste, thay appeared in five
great batells.*

*And as soone as the Scottes perceived my said Lordes to be withyn the daunger of thair
ordenance thay shote sharpely thair gonnes which wer verray great, and in like maner our
partye recounterde them, with thair ordenance, and notwithstanding that other our artillery
for warre couth doe noe good nor advantage to our army because they wer continually goyng
and advansyng vp towarde the said hilles and mountains, yit by the help of God, our gonnes
die soe breke and constreyn the Scotisshe great army, that some parte of thaim wer enforsed
to come doune the said hilles towarde our army, And my Lord Hawarde conceiving the great
power of the Scottes, sent to my said of Surrey his fader and required hym to advaunce his
rerewarde and to joine his wyng with his left wyng, for the Scottes wer of that might that
the vawarde was not of power nor abull to encounter thaim, My said Lorde of Surrey per-
fitely vunderstanding this with all spede and diligence, lustily, came forwarde and joined hym*

to the vawarde as afor required by my said Lord Hawarde, and was glad for necessite to make of two battalles oon good battell to aventure of the said five batelles.

And for so myche as the Scottes did kepe thaim seuerall in five batelles therefore my Lorde of Surrey and my Lord Hawarde sodenly wer constreyned and enforced to devide thair army in oder five batelles, and ells it was thought it shulde haue bene to thair great daunger and jeopardy.

Soe it was that the Lorde Chamberlaine of Scotlande being Capitaine of the first bataill of the Scottes, fiercely did sett vpon Mr Edmonde Hawarde Capitaine of th'uttermoste parte of the felde at the weste side, and between thaim was so cruell batell that many of our par-tye Chesshirmen and other did flee, and the said Maister Edmonde in maner left alon with-out soccour, and his standerde and berer of the same betten and hewed in peces, and hym self thrise strykyn doune to the grounde, how be it like a coragious and an hardy yong lusty gentilman he recoverd againe and faught hande to hande with oone Sir Davy Home, and slew him with his oune hande, and thus the said Maister Edmonde was in great perell and daunger till that the Lorde Dacre like a good and an hardy knyght releved and come vnto hym for his soccour.

The secunde batell came vpon my Lord Hawarde, The thirde batell wherynne was the King of Scottes and mooste parte of the noble men of his realme came fercely vpon my said Lord Surrey, which two batelles by the help of Allmyghtty God wer aftir a great conflict ven-quesshed, overcome, bettyn doune and put to flight, and few of thaim escaped with thair lyves, Sir Edward Stanley being at the vttermoste parte of the said rerewarde on th'Est par-tie, seing the fourth batelles redy to relief the said King of Scottes batell, coragiously and like a lusty and an hardy knyght, did sett vpon the same and overcame, and put to flight all the Scotts in the said batell And thus by the grace socour and help of Allmyghtty God victory was given to the realme of Englande, and all the Scotissh ordenance wonne and brought to Etell and Barwike in surtie.

In this batell the Scottes had many gret aduantages that is to witt, the high hilles and mountains, a great wynd with thaim, and sodden raine, all contrarie to our bowes and archers, It is not to be douted, but the Scotts faught manly, and wer determyned outhir to wynne the ffelde or to dye, they wer also as well appointed as was possible at all points with armes and harness, Soe that few of thaim wer slaine with arrows, how be it the billes did beat and hew thaim doune with some paine and daunger to Englisshmen.

The said Scottes wer soe plainly determynned to abide bataill and not to flee, that thay put frome thaym thair horses and also put of thair boitte and shois, and faught in the vampis of thair hoses every man for the moost parte with a kene and a sharp sper of v yerds long, and a target afor hym, And when thair speres failed and wer spent, then they faught with great and sharp swerdes, makying litle or noe noes without that that for the mooste parte, any of thaim wolde desir to be saved.

David Laing (ed.), 'A Contemporary Account of the Battle of Flodden, 9 September 1513: Hereafter ensue the Trewe Encountre or Batayle lately don between Englande and Scotlande: In Whiche Batayle the Scottsshe Kynge was slayne', *Proceedings of the Society of Antiquaries of Scotland*, vol. 7, March 1867, pp.147-151.

APPENDIX V

Extract from Hall's *Henry the VIII*

Then the Lord Admyrall perceyued foure greate battayles of the Scottes all on foote with long speres lyke moorishe pykes: whyche the Scottes furnished them warlike, and bent them to theim to the forwarde, whiche was conducted by the Lord Admirall, whiche perceyuynge that sent to hys Father the Erle of Surrey hys Agnus dei that honge at hys brest that in all hast he would ioyne battayll, euen wyth the bront or brest of the vantgarde: for the forward alone was not able to encountre the whole battayll of the Scottes, the erle perceyuynge well the saiynge of hys sonne, and seynge the Scottes ready to discende the hyll auaunsed hym selfe and hys people forwarde, and broughte theym egall in grounde wyth the forwarde on the left hande, euen at the bront or brest of the same at the foote of thehyll called Bramston, the Englishe army stretched east and west, and their backes northe, and the Scottes in the southe before theim on the forsayde hyll called Bramston. Then oute braste the ordinaunce on bothe sydes wyth fyre flamme and hydeous noyse, and the Master Gonner of the Englishe parte slewe the Master Gonner of Scotlande, and bet all hys men from theyr ordinaunce, so that the Scottishe ordynaunce did no harme too the Englishemen, but the Englishemens artyllerie shotte into the myddes of the Kynge battayll, and slew many persones, which seyng the kyng of Scottes and hys noble men, made the more haste too come too ioynyng, and so all the foure battayles in maner discended the hyl at once. And after that the shotte was done, whiche they defended withy Pauishes, they came to han-destrokes, and were encountered seuerally as you shall here.

Fyrst on the Englyshe syde next the west, was Syr Edmonde Hawarde knyghte, Marshall of the hoste chief Capitayne of a wyng of the ryghte hand of oure vantgarde, and was encoun-tryd with the Chamberlayne of Scotlande wyth hys battayle of sperys on foote, to the num-ber of ten thousande at the least, whiche foughte valiauntly, so that they by force caused the lytle wynge to flye, and the same Syr Edmonde thre tymes felled to the grounde, and left alone sauying his standarde berar, and tow of hys seruantes, too whome came Ihon Heron Bastarde sore hurte, saiynge there was neuer noble mans sonne so lyke too be loste as you be thys daye, for all my hurtes I shall lyue and dye wyth you, and there thesayde Syr Edmonde Hawarde was in a great daunger and ieopardie of hys lyfe, and hardelye escaped, and yet as he was goynge to the body of the vantgard he with Davy Home, and slew hym hys awn hande, and so came to the vantgarde.

Secondely, eastwarde from the sayde battayle was the Lorde Admyrall with the vantgarde, with whom encountred the Erles of Crafforde and Montroos, accompaignied with many lordes, knyghtes and gentelmen, all with sperys on foote, but the Lorde Admyrall and hys

203

compaignie acquyted them selfes so well, and that with pure fighting, that they brought to ground a great number, and both the Erles slayne.

Thirdely, eastwarde from the Lorde Admyrall was the Erle of Surrey, Capitayne generall, to whose standarde the Kynge of Scottes in hys awne person marched, beynge accompaigned wyth many bishoppes, erles, barons, knyghtes and gentelmen of the realme, with a great number of commons, all chosen men with speres on foote, whiche were the most assuredly harnessed that hath bene sene, and that the tallest and goodlyest personages with all, and they abode the most daungerous shot of arrowes, which sore them noyed, and yet except it hit them in some bare place it dyd them no hurt. After the shotte endyd, the battayll was cruell, none spared other and the Kynge hym self fought valiauntly. Oh what a noble and triumphaunt courage was thys for a kyng to fyghte in a battayll as a meane souldier: But what aualyed hys strong harnes, the puyssaunce of hys myghtie champions with whome he descended the hyll, in whome he soo much trusted that with hys stronge people and great number of men, he was able as he thought to haue vanquished that day the greatest prynce of the world, if he had ben there as the Erle of Surrey was, or els he thought to do such an hygh entreprice hym selfe in his person, that should surmount the enterprises of all other princes: but how soeuer it happened God gaue the stroke, and he was no more regarded then a poore souldier, for all went one way. So that of his awne battaill none escaped but syr William Scot knight his Chancelour, and syr Ihon forman knight, his seriaunt Porter, whiche were taken prisoners, and w great difficulty saued. This may be a great myrror to all prynces, how that they aduenter them selfes in such a battaii.

Forthely, eastward was Syr Edward Stanley knight, capitayn of the left wyng with the sayde erle, which clame vp to the toppe of the hyll called Bramston, or the Scottes wiste, and with him encountred the Erles of Huntley, Lenoux and Argile, with a great number of Scottes whiche were sore fought with all, whiche perceyuinge the Erle of Huntley toke a horse and saued hym selfe, if he had taryed he had bene likely to haue gone with his compaignie: such as fled, the sayde Syr Edward and his people folowed the ouer the same grounde, where the erles battell first ioyned, and founde the Scottes, whiche were by the erles battaill slayne before, and sodainly left the chase and fell a spoyling, and spoyled the Kyng of Scottes, and many that wer slayne in his battaill, but they knew him not, and found a Crosse and certayne thinges of his, by reason wherof some sayde that he was slayne by that wyng, whiche could not be true, for the prisoners of Scotlad testified that the Kinges battaill fought onely with the erles battels, but for a truthe this wyng did very valiauntly: wherefore it was thought that the said Syr Edward might that daye not haue bene missed.

All these four battels, in maner fought at one tyme, and were determined in effect littell in distance of the beginnyng and endynge of any of them one before the other, sauing that Syr Edward Stanley, which was the last that fought, for he came vp to the toppe of the hyll, and there fought with the Scottes valiauntly, and chaced them doune the hyll ouer that place, where the kynges battail ioyned. Beside these four battayles of the Scottes were twoo other battayls, whiche neuer came to hande strokes.

Edward Hall, *The Triumphant Reigne of Kyng Henry the VIII*, vol. I, London, 1904, pp.561–563.

APPENDIX VI

Extract from Piscottie's
Cronicles of Scotland

Then the trumpitis blew on everie syde and the wangairdis ioynitt togither, to wit, the Scottis wangaird, the Earle of Huntlie, the Lord Home, witht the Borderaris and contriemen to the number of 10,000, and on the wther syde, of Ingland the Lord Percie and the Lord Wastmureland witht the haill Borderaris and countriemen tharof in lyke maner, quho junitt cruellie on everie syde and faught crwellie witht uncertaine wictorie. Bot at last the Earle of Hunttleis Hieland men witht thair bowis and tua handit suordis wrocht sa manfullie that they defait the Inglischemen bot ony slaughter on thair syde; then the Earle of Huntlie and Lord Home blew thair trumpattis and convenit thair men agane to thair standartis. Be this the tua great battellis of Ingland come fordward wpoun the Kingis battell and ionitt awfullie at the sownd of the trumpit and faught furieouslie and lang quhill. Bot at last the King of Scottland defaitt them both.

Then the great battell of Ingland led be the Lord Halbert quho was wnder his father the Earle of Surray governour in that battell quho come furieouslie wpoun the King to the number of 20,000 men; bot the Kingis battell inconterid him crwellie and faught manfullie on both the saydis witht wncertane wictorie, quhill that the stremis of blude ran on ather syde so aboundantlie that all the fieldis and wateris was maid reid witht the conflewence thairof. The Earle of Huntlie then and the Lord of Home standand in ane rayit battell quho had win the wangaird affoir and few of thair men ether hurt or slaine, the Earle of Hunttlie desyrit at the Lord Home that he wald help the king and reskew him in his extremmitie, ffor he said he was ower sett witht multitud of men. Nochtwithtstanding, the Lord Home ansuerit the Earle of Huntlie in this maner, sayand, 'He dois weill that dois for him self; we haue faught our wangaird alreddie and win the samin thairfoir lat the laif do thair pairt as we'. The Earle of Huntlie ansuerit againe and said he could nocht suffer his natiue prince to be owercome witht his enemeis beffoir his ene, thairfor callit his men togither be sloghorne and sound of trumpit to haue passit to the king bot, or he come, all was defait on ether syde that few or nane was lewand nother on the Kingis pairt nor on the wther.

Robert Lindesay of Pitscottie, *The Historie and Cronicles of Scotland*, vol. I, Edinburgh, 1899, pp.270–272.

NOTES

PREFACE

1 Henry James (ed.), 'Account of the Battle of Flodden, Articules of the Bataille bitwix the Kynge of Scottes and therle of Surrey in Brankstone felde the 9 day of Septembre', in Henry James (ed.), *Facsimiles of National Manuscripts from William the Conqueror to Queen Anne*, Southampton, 1865, pt 2, pp.2–3.

2 David Laing (ed.), 'A Contemporary Account of the Battle of Flodden, 9th September 1513: Hereafter ensue the Trewe Encountre or Batayle lately don between Englande and Scotlande: In Whiche Batayle the Scottsshe Kynge was slayne', *Proceedings of the Society of Antiquaries of Scotland*, vol. 7, March 1867, p.145.

3 Edward Hall, *The Triumphant Reigne of Kyng Henry the VIII*, vol. I pp.95–113, London, 1904.

4 J.S. Brewer (ed.), *Letters and Papers, Foreign and Domestic, of the Reign of Henry VIII*, vol. I (1509–1514), London, 1862, nos2283, 2284; James, *National Manuscripts*, pp.6–8.

5 Ranald Nicholson, *Scotland: The Later Middle Ages*, Edinburgh, 1974; Leslie J. Macfarlane, *William Elphinstone and the Kingdom of Scotland, 1431–1514: The Struggle for Order*, Aberdeen, 1985.

6 Norman MacDougall, *James IV*, Edinburgh, 1997.

7 Alfred H. Burne, The *Battlefields of Britain*, London, 1996.

8 Ardant du Picq, *Battle Studies*, US Army War College, 1983.

9 John Keegan, *The Face of Battle*, London, 1988, p.84.

I: A WEB OF INTRIGUE

1 Hall, *Kyng Henry the VIII*, p.545.

2 Brewer, *Letters and Papers*, no.4351; G. Gregory Smith (ed.), *Scottish History by Contemporary Writers, no.1: The Days of James IV, 1488–1513*, London, 1900, p.146.

3 Hall, *Kyng Henry the VIII*, p.545.

4 Ibid.

5 S.B. Chrimes, *Henry VII*, London, 1972, pp.272–297.

6 J.J. Scarisbrick, *Henry VIII*, London, 1970, pp.4–6.

7 Polydore Vergil, Denys Hay (ed.), *Anglica Historia*, London, 1950, p.161.

8 Scarisbrick, *Henry VIII*, pp.21–24.

9 Ibid, p.27.

10 Charles Cruickshank, *Henry VIII and the Invasion of France*, Stroud, 1994, p.4.

11 Ibid, pp.4–5.

12 Scarisbrick, *Henry VIII*, p.34.

13 Niccolò Machiavelli, *The Prince*, Oxford, 1984 (written in 1513 and first published in 1532), p.73.

14 Scarisbrick, *Henry VIII*, pp.33–34.

15 Cruickshank, *Henry VIII and the Invasion of France*, p.9.

16 MacDougall, *James IV*, p.262; Nicholson, *Scotland*, p.598.

17 Nicholson, *Scotland*, p.541.

18 Ibid, pp.541–549.

19 G.A. Bergenroth (ed.), *Calendar of Letters, Despatches and State Papers relating to the negotiations between England and Spain*, vol. I, no.210.

20 MacDougall, *James IV*, pp.200–208; Nicholson, *Scotland*, p.594.

21 MacDougall, *James IV*, p.207.

22 Ibid, pp.210–219.

23 Ibid, p.197.

24 Nicholson, *Scotland*, p.592.

25 David H. Caldwell, 'Royal Patronage of Arms and Armour Making in Fifteenth and Sixteenth Century Scotland', in David H. Caldwell (ed.) *Scottish Weapons and Fortifications 1100–1800*, Edinburgh, 1981, p.76.

26 Ibid, pp.592–594.

27 MacDougall, *James IV*, p.243.

28 Norman MacDougall, 'The Greatest Scheip That Ever Saillit in Ingland or France', in Norman MacDougall (ed.), *Scotland and War AD 79–1918*, p.45.

29 MacDougall, *James IV*, p.233; Margaret Rule, *The Mary Rose: Excavation and Raising of Henry VIII's Flagship*, p.13, London, 1982.

30 Ibid.

31 MacDougall, *James IV*, pp.118–133.

32 Nicholson, *Scotland*, p.551.

33 MacDougall, *James IV*, pp.133–141.

34 Bergenroth, *Calendar of Letters, Spain*, vol. I, no.210.

35 MacDougall, *James IV*, p.249.

36 Ibid, pp.258–259.

37 Smith, *The Days of James IV*, p.134.

38 Brewer, *Letters and Papers*, No.4351; Smith, *The Days of James IV*, p.144; MacDougall, *James IV*, p.252.

39 Hall, *Henry VIII*, p.525.

40 MacDougall, *James IV*, p.203.

41 Robert Lindesay of Pitscottie, *The Historie and Cronicles of Scotland*, vol. I, Edinburgh, 1899, p.256.

42 Machiavelli, *The Prince*, p.75.

43 Brewer, *Letters and Papers*, vol.I, pt 2, no.2157.

44 Smith, *The Days of James IV*, p.127.

45 MacDougall, *James IV*, pp.259–260; Nicholson, *Scotland*, p.597.

46 Smith, *The Days of James IV*, pp.129–130.

47 Nicholson, *Scotland*, p.600.

48 Scarisbrick, *Henry VIII*, p.34.

49 Smith, *The Days of James IV*, p.137.

50 Brewer, *Letters and Papers*, no. 2291.

51 Smith, *The Days of James IV*, p.126.

52 Machiavelli, *The Prince*, p.76.

53 Macfarlane, *Elphinstone*, p.429.

54 Smith, *The Days of James IV*, pp.137–139.

55 Ibid.

56 Pitscottie, *Historie and Cronicles of Scotland*, p.256.

2: THE ARMIES OF 1513

1 H.C.B. Rogers, *Artillery through the Ages*, London, 1971, p.24.

2 Charles Oman, *A History of the Art of War in the Sixteenth Century*, London, 1937, p.53.

3 Clifford J. Rogers, *The Military Revolution Debate: Readings on the Transformation of Early Modern Europe*, Oxford, 1995.

4 James, 'Articules of the Bataille', in James, *National Manuscripts*, p.2.

5   This link was first explored by W. Mackay Mackenzie, *The Secret of Flodden*, Edinburgh, 1931.

6   Frederic J. Baumgarter, *From Spear to Flintlock: A History of War in Europe and the Middle East to the French Revolution*, New York, 1991, p.158.

7   Ibid, pp.157–158.

8   Ibid, pp.158–159.

9   Douglas Miller, *The Swiss at War: 1300–1500*, London, 1979, p.13.

10 Oman, *The Art of War in the Sixteenth Century*, p.63.

11 Baumgarter, *From Spear to Flintlock*, pp.161–162.

12 Phillipe de Commynes, *The Universal Spider*, London, 1973, p.212.

13 Miller, *The Swiss at War*, p.37.

14 Baumgarter, *From Spear to Flintlock*, p.161.

15 Miller, *The Swiss at War*, pp.13–14

16 Ibid.

17 Baumgarter, *From Spear to Flintlock*, p.161.

18 Miller, *The Swiss at War*, pp.16–17.

19 Niccolò Machiavelli, *The Art of War*, New York, 1965 (first published in 1521), p.86.

20 Miller, *The Swiss at War*, pp.37–38.

21 Quoted in John Vincent, *Switzerland at the Beginning of the Sixteenth Century*, New York, 1974, pp.16–17.

22 Baumgarter, *From Spear to Flintlock*, p.161.

23 Machiavelli, *The Art of War*, p.47.

24 Oman, *The Art of War in the Sixteenth Century*, pp.42–43.

25 Ibid, p.64.

26 Oman, *The Art of War in the Sixteenth Century*, p.65.

27 Oman, *The Art of War in the Sixteenth Century*, pp.44–45.

28 Douglas Miller, *The Landsknechts*, London, 1976, p.3.

29 Miller, *The Landsknechts*, pp.6–7.

30 Oman, *Middle Ages*, p.562.

31 Oman, *A History of the Art of War: The Middle Ages to the Fourteenth Century*, London, 1898, pp.565–568.

32 Ibid, pp.570–580.

33 Ibid, p.588.

34 Ibid, pp.586–587.

35 Ibid, p.587.

36 Robert B.K. Stevenson, 'The Return of Mons Meg From London, 1828–1829', in Caldwell, *Scottish Weapons*, p.419.

37 Nicholas Michael, *Armies of Medieval Burgundy: 1364–1477*, London, 1983, pp.10–16.

38 Ibid, p.6.

39 David H. Caldwell, 'Some Notes on Scottish Axes and Long Shafted Weapons', in Caldwell, *Scottish Weapons*, p.254.

40 Hall, *Kyng Henry the VIII*, p.555.

41 Brewer, *Letters and Papers*, no.2291.

42 R.K. Hannay, *Acts of the Lords of Scotland in Public Affairs, 1501–44*, Edinburgh, 1932, p.2.

43 David Eltis, *The Military Revolution in Sixteenth Century Europe*, London, 1995, p.12.

44 Ibid.

45 Caldwell, 'Royal Patronage', in Caldwell, *Scottish Weapons*, p.84.

46 Stevenson, 'Mons Meg', in Caldwell, *Scottish Weapons*, p.419.

47 O.F. Hogg, *English Artillery, 1326–1716*, London, 1963, p.10.

48 David H. Caldwell, 'Mons Meg Original Carriage and the Carvings of Artillery in Edinburgh Castle', in Caldwell, *Scottish Weapons*, p.437.

49 Hogg, *English Artillery*, p.12.

50 Ibid, p.21.

51 Rogers, *Artillery through the Ages*, p.24.

52 Mackenzie, *The Secret of Flodden*, pp.59–61.

53 Rogers, *Artillery through the Ages*, p.30.

54 The term 'gun stone' remained in common use long after gunners had abandoned stone shot.

55 J.D. Mackie, 'The English Army at Flodden', in *Miscellany of the Scottish History Society*, vol. VIII, Edinburgh, 1951, pp.43–44.

56 Hall, *Kyng Henry the VIII*, p.557.

57 James, 'Articules of the Bataille' in James, *National Manuscripts*, p.3.

58 Pitscottie, *Historie and Cronicles of Scotland*, p.262, 263, 270.

59 Gervase Phillips, *The Anglo-Scots Wars, 1513–1550*, Woodbridge, 1999, p.150.

60 Ibid, p.182.

61 Mackie, 'The English Army at Flodden', pp.48–49.

62 Quoted in Peter Young and John Adair, *Hastings to Culloden*, p.104–105.

63 Gibert John Millar, *Tudor Mercenaries and Auxiliaries, 1485–1547*, Charlottesville, 1980, p.45.

64 Ibid, p.44.

65 Laing, 'The Trewe Encountre', p.145.

66 Guest, *British Battles*, p.65.

67 Harold A. Dillon, 'Arms and Armour at Westminster, the Tower, and Greenwich, 1547', *Archaeologia*, vol. 51, 1888, p.235.

68 Ken and Denise Guest, *British Battles*, London, 1996, p.66.

69 Clive Bartlett, *English Longbowman: 1330–1515*, London, 1995, pp.26–27; Keegan, *The Face of Battle*, p.84.

70 Oman, *Middle Ages*, p.595–596.

71 Keegan, *The Face of Battle*, pp.75–76.

72 Hogg, *English Artillery*, p.213.

73 Ibid, pp.102, 214.

74 H.L. Blackmore, *The Armouries of the Tower of London: I Ordnance*, London, 1976, p.4.

75 Hogg, *English Artillery*, p.16.

76 Mackie, 'The English Army at Flodden', p.63.

77 Ibid, pp.55–56.

78 Ibid, pp.49–53.

79 Ibid, pp.60–65.

80 Ibid, pp.65–69.

81 Ibid, p.84.

82 Cruickshank, *Henry VIII and the Invasion of France*, p.173.

83 Mackie, 'The English Army at Flodden', pp.57–58.

84 Ibid, p.65.

85 Ian F. Baird (ed.), *Scotish Feilde and Flodden Feilde: Two Flodden Poems*, London, 1982, p.13.

86 Ibid, p.9.

87 Graham Maddocks, *Liverpool Pals: A History of the 17th 18th 19th & 20th Battalions The King's (Liverpool Regiment) 1914–1919*, Leo Cooper, 1996, pp.23–24.

88 Ibid, pp.32–33.

3: JAMES IV'S INVASION

1 Cruickshank, *Henry VIII and the Invasion of France*, p.16.

2 Ibid, p.178.

3 Hall, *Kyng Henry the VIII*, p.555

4 Ibid.

5 Mackie, *'The English Army at Flodden'*, pp.76–77.

6 Hall, *Kyng Henry the VIII*, p.556.

7 MacDougall, *James IV*, p.267.

8 Pitscottie, *Historie and Cronicles of Scotland*, pp.257–258.

9 Ibid, pp.258–259.

10 MacDougall, *James IV*, p.268.

11 Ibid, p.125.

12 Hall, *Kyng Henry the VIII*, p.556.

13 Ibid.

14 Brewer, *Letters and Papers*, no.4403.

15 Pitscottie, *Historie and Cronicles of Scotland*, pp.260–261.

16 Mackie, 'The English Army at Flodden', p.46.

17 Cruickshank, *Henry VIII and the Invasion of France*, pp.103–107.

18 MacDougall, *James IV*, p.272.

19 Ibid, p.271.

20 Hall, *Kyng Henry the VIII*, p.556.

21 Andrew Saunders, *Norham Castle*, London, 1998, p.20.

22 Ibid, pp.3–16.

23 Ibid, p.16.

24 Ibid, p.6.

25 Ibid.

26 Hall, *Kyng Henry the VIII*, p.557.

27 Ibid.

28 Brewer, *Letters and Papers*, no.2284.

29 Ibid, no.2279.

30 MacDougall, *James IV*, pp.272–273.

31 Pitscottie, *Historie and Cronicles of Scotland*, pp.262–263.

32 Hall, *Kyng Henry the VIII*, p.558.

33 Pitscottie, *Historie and Cronicles of Scotland*, p.264.

34 Quoted in Charles Kightly, *Flodden: The Anglo-Scottish War of 1513*, London, 1975, p.9.

35 MacDougall, *James IV*, p.273.

36 Mackie, 'The English Army at Flodden', pp.46–47.

37 Ibid, pp.47–49.

38 Hall, *Kyng Henry the VIII*, p.557.

39 Ibid; Mackie, 'The English Army at Flodden', p.81.

40 Hall, *Kyng Henry the VIII*, p.557.

41 Ibid.

42 Ibid.

43 Ibid; Laing, 'The Trewe Encountre', p.145.

44 Ibid.

45 Ibid.

46 Ibid.

47 Ibid.

48 Ibid.

49 Hall, *Kyng Henry VIII*, p.557.

50 Ibid, p.558.

51 Ibid.

52 Ibid, p.559.

53 Ibid, p.560.

54 Laing, 'The Trewe Encountre', p.146.

55 Hall, *Kyng Henry the VIII*, p.560.

56 Oman, *The Art of War in the Sixteenth Century*, pp.132–133.

57 Oman, *Middle Ages*, pp.570–580.

58 Ibid, pp.563–565, 570–580

59 Hall, *Kyng Henry the VIII*, p.560.

60 Ibid.

61 Laing, 'The Trewe Encountre', p.146.

62 Ibid.

63 Baird, *Scotish Feilde and Flodden Feilde*, p.12.

64 Ibid, p.10.

65 Hall, *Kyng Henry the VIII*, p.561.

66 Ibid, p.268.

67 Ibid, p.269.

68 Bergenroth, *Calendar of Letters, Spain*, vol. I, no.210.

69 Ibid.

70 Oman, *Middle Ages*, p.387.

71 Burne, *Battlefields*, p.123.

72 Charles Sanford Terry, *John Graham of Claverhouse, Viscount of Dundee*, London, 1905, p.287.

73 Pitscottie, *Historie and Cronicles of Scotland*, p.270.

74 Ibid.

75 Hall, *Kyng Henry the VIII*, p.561.

76 Ibid.

77 Baird, *Scotish Feilde and Flodden Feilde*, p.12.

78 Hall, *Kyng Henry the VIII*, p.561.

79 Ibid.

80 Pitscottie, *Historie and Cronicles of Scotland*, pp.270–271.

81 Hall, *Kyng Henry the VIII*, p.563.

82 Laing, 'The Trewe Encountre', p.147.

83 James, ' Articules of the Bataille' in James, *National Manuscripts*, p.2.

84 Ibid.

85 *La Rotta de Scocesi* translated and printed in W. Mackay Mackenzie, *The*

Secret of Flodden, Edinburgh, 1931, pp.115–122.

86 Machiavelli, *The Art of War*, p.86.

87 Hall, *Kyng Henry the VIII*, p.562.

88 Laing, 'The Trewe Encountre', p.147.

89 F.W.D. Brie (ed.), *The Brut or Chronicles of England,* London, 1906, pp.211–212.

90 Oman, *Middle Ages*, p.580.

91 Laing, 'The Trewe Encountre', p.147.

92 Hall, *Kyng Henry the VIII*, p.561.

93 Ibid.

94 James, ' Articules of the Bataille' in James, *National Manuscripts*, p.2.

95 Hall, *Kyng Henry the VIII*, p.561.

96 Laing, 'The Trewe Encountre', p.148.

97 Ibid.

98 James, ' Articules of the Bataille' in James, *National Manuscripts*, p.2.

99 Pitscottie, *Historie and Cronicles of Scotland*, p.270.

4: THE FIELD OF FLODDEN

1 James, ' Articules of the Bataille' in James, *National Manuscripts*, p.2.

2 Pitscottie, *Historie and Cronicles*, p.270.

3 Hall, *Kyng Henry the VIII*, p.561.

4 Laing, 'The Trewe Encountre', p.147.

5 Hall, *Kyng Henry the VIII*, p.561.

6 Borthwick cast many bells after Flodden, including two, dated 1528, for St Magnus Cathedral, Kirkwall, Caldwell, 'Royal Patronage', in Caldwell, *Scottish Weapons*, p.77.

7 B.P. Hughes, *Firepower: Weapons Effectiveness on the Battlefield, 1630–1850*, London, 1974, pp.29–33.

8 John Leslie, *The Historie of Scotland*, Edinburgh, 1895, p.145.

9 Hughes, *Firepower*, pp.29–33.

10 Hogg, *English Artillery*, p.20; Hughes, *Firepower*, p.35.

11 Hall, *Kyng Henry the VIII*, p.561.

12 Ibid.

13 Oman, *Middle Ages*, p.587.

14 Machiavelli, *The Art of War*, p.97.

15 Hall, *Kyng Henry the VIII*, pp.561–562.

16 Laing, 'The Trewe Encountre', pp.147–148.

17 James, ' Articules of the Bataille' in James, *National Manuscripts*, p.2.

18 Machiavelli, *The Art of War*, p109.

19 Hall, *Kyng Henry the VIII*, pp.562–563.

20 Ibid, pp.561–562.

21 Oman, *The Art of War in the Sixteenth Century*, p.69.

22 Brian Bond and Nigel Cave (ed.), *Haig: A Reappraisal Seventy Years On*, London, 1999.

23 Kenneth Macksey, *Rommel: Battles and Campaigns*, London, 1979.

24 Bergenroth, *Calendar of Letters, Spain*, vol. I, no.210.

25 Laing, 'The Trewe Encountre', p.151.

26 Ibid.

27 Ibid.

28 Ibid, p.150.

29 Hall, *Kyng Henry the VIII*, p.562.

30 James, ' Articules of the Bataille' in James, *National Manuscripts*, p.2.

31 Baird, *Scotish Feilde and Flodden Feilde*, p.13.

32 Pitscottie, *Historie and Cronicles of Scotland*, p.270.

33 Baird, *Scotish Feilde and Flodden Feilde*, p.14.

34 Ibid, p.13.

35 Laing, 'The Trewe Encountre', p.148.

36 Hall, *Kyng Henry the VIII*, p.562.

37 *Articules of the Bataille*.

38 Pitscottie, *Historie and Cronicles of Scotland*, p.271.

39 Ibid, pp.271–272.

40 MacDougall, *James IV*, p.299.

41 Hall, *Kyng Henry the VIII*, p.561.

42 James, ' Articules of the Bataille' in James, *National Manuscripts*, p.2.

43 du Picq, *Battle Studies*, p.86; Keegan,

The Face of Battle, p.86.

44 Laing, 'The Trewe Encountre', p.148.

45 Brewer, *Letters and Papers*, no.2283.

46 *La Rotta de Scocesi* in Mackenzie, *The Secret of Flodden*, p.34.

47 Laing, 'The Trewe Encountre', p.151.

48 James, *Facsimiles of National Manuscipts*, pt 2, pp.4–8.

49 du Picq, *Battle Studies*, p.90.

50 *La Rotta de Scocesi* in Mackenzie, *The Secret of Flodden*, p.35.

51 Laing, 'The Trewe Encountre', p.150.

52 du Picq, *Battle Studies*, p.89.

53 Ibid.

54 James, ' Articules of the Bataille' in James, *National Manuscripts*, p.2.

55 James, *Facsimiles of National Manuscipts*, pt 2, pp.4–8.

56 Kightly, *Flodden*, p.45.

57 Leslie, *Historie of Scotland*, p.95.

58 James, *National Manuscripts*, pt 2, p.6; *Letters and Papers*, Ruthal to Wolsey, no.4461.

59 Laing, 'The Trewe Encountre', p.150.

60 Ibid.

61 Ibid.

62 James, *National Manuscripts*, pt 2, p.6; *Letters and Papers*, Ruthal to Wolsey, no.4461.

63 Laing, 'The Trewe Encountre', p.148.

64 James, ' Articules of the Bataille' in James, *National Manuscripts*, p.2.

65 Laing, 'The Trewe Encountre', p.148.

66 Baird, *Flodden Field* in *Scotish Feilde and Flodden Feilde*, p.46.

67 Hall, *Kyng Henry the VIII*, p.562.

68 Ibid, p.563.

69 James, 'Articules of the Bataille' in James, *National Manuscripts*, p.3.

70 Baird, *Scotish Feilde and Flodden Feilde*, p.15.

71 Hall, *Kyng Henry the VIII*, pp.563–564.

72 Laing, 'The Trewe Encountre', p.151.

73 Brewer, *Letters and Papers*, Ruthal to Wolsey, no.2283.

74 Hall, *Kyng Henry the VIII*, p.564.

75 Laing, 'The Trewe Encountre', p.151–152.

76 Hall, *Kyng Henry the VIII*, p.564.

77 Baird, *Scotish Feilde and Flodden Feilde*, p.16.

5: THE 'FLOWERS OF THE FOREST'

1 Pitscottie, *Historie and Cronicles of Scotland*, p.271.

2 Hall, *Kyng Henry the VIII*, p.564.

3 Brewer, *Letters and Papers*, Ruthal to Wolsey, no.2284.

4 Robert Jones, *The Battle of Flodden Field fought September 9, 1513*, Edinburgh, 1864.

5 James, ' Articules of the Bataille' in James, *National Manuscripts*, p.3.

6 Hall, *Kyng Henry the VIII*, p. 563.

7 Mackie, 'The English Army at Flodden', p.82.

8 James, *Facsimiles of National Manuscripts*, pt 2, p.6.

9 Sir David Lindsay, *The Testament and Complaynt of the Papingo*, Laing's edition, I, l.79, p.486.

10 J.M.Winter, *The Great War and the British People*, London, 1985, p.99.

11 Ibid, pp.97–99.

12 MacDougall, *James IV*, p.276.

13 Oman, *The Art of War in the Sixteenth Century*, p.318.

14 Hall, *Kyng Henry the VIII*, p.564; Laing, 'The Trewe Encountre', p.150.

15 Nicholson, *Scotland*, p.605.

16 Hall, *Kyng Henry the VIII*, p.564.

17 Ibid.

18 Ibid.

19 Ibid.

20 Brewer, *Letters and Papers*, no.2283.

21 Macfarlane, *Elphinstone*, p.431.

22 John Stow, *The Survey of London*, London, 1633, p.539.

23 Hall, *Kyng Henry the VIII*, p.564.

24 James, *National Manuscripts*, pt 2, p.8.

25 Mackie, 'The English army at Flodden', pp.65–69.

26 Baird, *Scotish Feilde and Flodden Feilde*, p.16.

27 Vergil *Anglica Historia*, pp.219–220.

28 Brewer, *Letters and Papers*, no.2286.

29 Smith, *The Days of James IV*, pp.179–180.

30 Lord Cullen, *The Walls of Edinburgh*, Cockburn Association, 1988; W. Bryce Moir, 'The Flodden Wall of Edinburgh', in *The Book of the Old Edinburgh Club*, vol. II, 1909, pp.61–79.

31 Baird, *Scotish Feilde and Flodden Feilde*, p.16.

32 MacDougall, 'The Greatest Scheip', in MacDougall, *Scotland and War*, p.56.

33 Gordon Donaldson, *Scotland: James V to James VII*, Edinburgh, 1971, pp.17–18.

34 Donaldson, *James V to James VII*, pp.18–19; Macfarlane, *Elphinstone*, p.431.

35 Donaldson, *James V to James VII*, p.32.

36 Ibid, pp.18–20.

37 Ibid, pp.31–32.

38 Scarisbrick, *Henry VIII*, pp.39–40.

39 J.J. Bagley, *The Earls of Derby, 1485–1985*, London, 1985, p.17.

40 Cruickshank, *Henry VIII and the Invasion of France*, p.107.

41 Scarisbrick, *Henry VIII* , p.54.

42 Ibid, pp.38–39.

43 Quoted in Peter Young and John Adair, *Hastings to Culloden*, pp.104–105.

44 Donaldson, *James V to James VII*, pp.20–21.

45 Phillips, *The Anglo-Scots Wars*, pp.150–153.

46 Maria Perry, *The Sisters of Henry VIII*, London, 1998, pp.170–171.

47 Pitscottie, *Historie and Cronicles of Scotland*, p.258, 260–261, 262–263.

48 Ibid, p.272.

49 Ibid, p.273.

50 Leslie, *The Historie of Scotland*, pp.95–96.

51 Roger Ascham, *Toxophilus*, London, 1902.

52 Baird, *Scotish Feilde and Flodden Feilde*.

53 Arthur Quiller-Couch (ed.), *The Oxford Book of English Verse: 1250–1900*, no.466.

54 Sir Walter Scott, *The Poetical Works of Sir Walter Scott*, Edinburgh, 1853; J.H. Alexander, *Marmion: Studies in Interpretation and Composition*, Salzburg, 1981.

55 William E. Ayton, *Ayton's Edinburgh After Flodden*, London, 1890.

56 T. Craig Brown, *Flodden Traditions of Selkirk*, Edinburgh, 1913.

57 Mackenzie, *The Secret of Flodden*, p.21.

58 Pitscottie, *Historie and Cronicles of Scotland*, p.276.

59 Sir Walter Scott, *The Tales of a Grandfather: Being the History of Scotland from the Earliest Period to the Close of the Rebellion 1745–46*, London, 1898, p.220, 224.

60 David H. Caldwell, 'The Battle of Pinkie, in MacDougall, *Scotland and War*, p.61.

61 Vergil, *Anglica Historia*, p.221.

62 Hall, *Kyng Henry the VIII*, p.562.

63 Cruickshank, *Henry VIII and the Invasion of France*, p.1.

64 Ibid, pp.1–2.

BIBLIOGRAPHY

PRIMARY PRINTED SOURCES

Ascham, Roger, *Toxophilus*, London, 1902.

Baird, Ian F. (ed.), *Scotish Feilde and Flodden Feilde: Two Flodden Poems*, London, 1982.

Bergenroth, G.A. (ed.), *Calendar of Letters, Despatches and State Papers relating to the negotiations between England and Spain*, London, 1862.

Brewer, J.S. (ed.), *Letters and Papers, Foreign and Domestic, of the Reign of Henry VIII*, vol. I (1509–1514), London, 1862.

Brie, F.W.D. (ed.), *The Brut or Chronicles of England,* London, 1906.

De Commynes, Phillipe, *The Universal Spider*, London, 1973.

Hall, Edward, *The Triumphant Reigne of Kyng Henry the VIII*, vol. I., London, 1904.

Hannay, R.K. (ed.), *Acts of the Lords of Scotland in Public Affairs, 1501–44*, Edinburgh, 1932.

James, Henry (ed.), 'Account of the Battle of Flodden, Articules of the Bataille bitwix the Kynge of Scottes and therle of Surrey in Brankstone felde the 9 day of Septembre', in Henry James (ed.), *Facsimiles of National Manuscripts from William the Conqueror to Queen Anne*, Southampton, 1865.

Laing, David (ed.), 'A Contemporary Account of the Battle of Flodden, 9 September 1513': Hereafter ensue the Trewe Encountre or Batayle lately don between Englande and Scotlande: In Whiche Batayle the Scottsshe Kynge was slayne', *Proceedings of the Society of Antiquaries of Scotland*, vol. 7, March 1867.

Laing, David (ed.), *The Poetical Works of Sir David Lindsay of the Mount,* Edinburgh, 1879.

Leslie, John, *The Historie of Scotland*, Edinburgh, 1895.

Lindesay of Pitscottie, Robert, *The Historie and Cronicles of Scotland*, vol. I., Edinburgh, 1899.

Machiavelli, Niccolò, *The Art of War*, New York, 1965.
The Prince, Oxford, 1984.

Skelton, John, *A Ballade of the Scottyshe Kinge*, London, 1882.

Smith, G. Gregory (ed.), *Scottish History By Contemporary Writers, no. 1: The Days of James IV, 1488–1513*, London, 1900.

Stow, John, *The Survey of London*, London, 1633.

Talbot White, John (ed.), *Death of a King: being extracts from contemporary accounts of the Battle of Branxton Moor, September 1513, commonly known as Flodden Field, wherein was slain James IV, King of Scotland*, Tragara Press, Edinburgh, 1970.

Vergil, Polydore, Denys Hay (ed.), *Anglica Historia*, London, 1950.

Wood, Marguerite (ed.), *Flodden papers: Diplomatic correspondence between the courts of France and Scotland 1507–1517*, Edinburgh, 1933.

Bibliography

SECONDARY SOURCES

Alexander, J.H., *Marmion: Studies in Interpretation and Composition*, Salzburg, 1981.

Ayton, William E., *Ayton's Edinburgh After Flodden*, London, 1890.

Bagley, J.J., *The Earls of Derby, 1485–1985*, London, 1985.

Bartlett, Clive, *English Longbowman: 1330–1515*, London, 1995.

Baumgarter, Frederic J., *From Spear to Flintlock: A History of War in Europe and the Middle East to the French Revolution*, New York, 1991.

Blackmore, H.L., *The Armouries of the Tower of London: I Ordnance*, London, 1976.

Blair, Claude, *European Armour*, London, 1979.

Bond, Brian and Cave, Nigel (ed.), *Haig: A Reappraisal Seventy Years On*, London, 1999.

Bryce Moir, W., 'The Flodden Wall of Edinburgh', in *The Book of the Old Edinburgh Club*, vol. II, 1909.

Burne, Alfred H., *The Battlefields of Britain*, London, 1996.

Caldwell, David H. (ed.) *Scottish Weapons and Fortifications 1100–1800*, Edinburgh, 1981.

Chrimes, S.B., *Henry VII*, London, 1972.

Craig Brown, T., *Flodden traditions of Selkirk*, Edinburgh, 1913.

Cruickshank, Charles, *Henry VIII and the Invasion of France*, Stroud, 1994.

Cullen, Lord, *The Walls of Edinburgh*, Cockburn Association, 1988.

Cummins, Mary, *Shadow over Flodden*, London, 1988.

Dillon, Harold A., 'Arms and Armour at Westminster, the Tower, and Greenwich, 1547', *Archaeologia*, vol. 51, 1888.

Donaldson, Gordon, *Scotland: James V to James VII*, Edinburgh, 1971.

du Picq, Ardant, *Battle Studies*, US Army War College, 1983.

Elliot, Fitzwilliam Andrew, *The Battle of Flodden and the Raids of 1513*, Edinburgh, 1911.

Eltis, David, *The Military Revolution in Sixteenth Century Europe*, London, 1995.

Fidler, Kathleen, *Flodden Field, September 9 1513*, London, 1971.

Guest, Ken and Denise, *British Battles*, London, 1996.

Gush, George, *Renaissance Armies, 1480-1650*, Cambridge, 1978.

Hardy, R., *Longbow*, London, 1976.

Hogg, O.F., *English Artillery, 1326–1716*, London, 1963.

Hughes, B.P., *Firepower: Weapons Effectiveness on the Battlefield, 1630–1850*, London, 1974.

Jones, Robert, *The Battle of Flodden Field fought September 9, 1513*, Edinburgh, 1864.

Keegan, John, *The Face of Battle*, London, 1988.

Kightly, Charles, *Flodden: The Anglo-Scottish War of 1513*, London, 1975.

Leather, G.F.T., *New Light on Flodden*, Edinburgh, 1937.

Lomas, Richard, *County of Conflict: Northumberland from Conquest to Civil War*, East Linton, 1996.

Macdonald Fraser, George, *The Steel Bonnets*, London, 1989.

MacDougall, Norman (ed.), *Scotland and War AD 79--1918*, Edinburgh, 1991.

James IV, Edinburgh, 1997.

Macfarlane, Leslie J., *William Elphinstone and the Kingdom of Scotland, 1431–1514: The Struggle for Order*,

Aberdeen, 1985.

Mackay Mackenzie, W., *The Secret of Flodden; with 'The rout of the Scots', a translation of the contemporary Italian poem La Rotta de Scocesi*, Edinburgh, 1931.

Mackenzie, D.M., *King's Henchmen, A romance of the time of Flodden*, London, 1940.

Mackie, J.D., 'The English Army at Flodden', in *Miscellany of the Scottish History Society*, vol. VIII Edinburgh, 1951.
   King James IV of Scotland, Edinburgh, 1958.
   The English Army at Flodden, Miscellany of the Scottish History Society, vol. VIII p.49, Edinburgh, 1951.

Macksey, Kenneth, *Rommel: Battles and Campaigns*, London, 1979.

Maclaren, David Shaw Moray, *If Freedom Fail: Bannockburn, Flodden, the Union*, Edinburgh, 1964.

Maddocks, Graham, *Liverpool Pals: A History of the 17th 18th 19th & 20th Battalions The King's (Liverpool Regiment) 1914–1919*, Leo Cooper, 1996.

Michael, Nicholas, *Armies of Medieval Burgundy: 1364–1477*, London, 1983.

Millar, Gibert John, *Tudor Mercenaries and Auxiliaries, 1485–1547*, Charlottesville, 1980.

Miller, Douglas, *The Landsknechts*, London, 1976.

Miller, Douglas, *The Swiss at War: 1300–1500*, London, 1979.

Nicholson, Ranald, *Scotland: the Later Middle Ages*, Edinburgh, 1974.

Oman, Charles, *The Art of War in the Sixteenth Century*, London, 1937.

Oman, Charles, *A History of the Art of War: The Middle Ages to the Fourteenth Century*, London, 1898.

Perry, Maria, *The Sisters of Henry VIII*, London, 1998.

Phillips, Gervase, *The Anglo-Scots Wars, 1513–1550*, Woodbridge, 1999.

Quiller-Couch, Arthur (ed.), *The Oxford Book of English Verse: 1250–1900*.

Rae, Thomas, *The Administration of the Scottish Frontier, 1513–1603*, Edinburgh, 1966.

Rogers, Clifford J., *The Military Revolution Debate: Readings on the Transformation of Early Modern Europe*, Oxford, 1995.

Rogers, H.C.B., *Artillery through the Ages*, London, 1971.

Rule, Margaret, *The Mary Rose: Excavation and Raising of Henry VIII's Flagship*, London, 1982.

Saunders, Andrew, *Norham Castle*, London, 1998.

Scarisbrick, J.J., *Henry VIII*, London, 1970.

Scott, Sir Walter, *The Poetical Works of Sir Walter Scott*, Edinburgh, 1853.
   The Tales of a Grandfather: Being the History of Scotland from the Earliest Period to the Close of the Rebellion 1745–46, London, 1898.

Sutcliffe, Halliwell, *Crimson Field: A Flodden Tale*, London, 1916.

Terry, Charles Sanford, *John Graham of Claverhouse, Viscount of Dundee*, London, 1905.

Vickers, K.H., *History of Northumberland*, London, 1922.

Vincent, John, *Switzerland at the Beginning of the Sixteenth Century*, New York, 1974.

Winter, J.M., *The Great War and the British People*, London, 1985.

Young, Peter and Adair, John, *Hastings to Culloden*, London, 1964.

LIST OF ILLUSTRATIONS

Copyright: GW: Geoffrey Wheeler, NB: Niall Barr, TA: Tempus Archive

Picture research by Geoffrey Wheeler, with thanks for additional material and information to Pete Armstrong; Dave Fiddimore; Marilyn Garabet; Alison and Richard Gough; Phillip Jackson; Lorraine Pickering and C.E.J. Smith.

PICTURES IN THE TEXT

PICTURE SECTIONS

11 Perkin Warbeck. GW.

12 A sketch of Margaret Tudor, Recueil d'Arras. GW.

13 Thomas Howard, 2nd Duke of Norfolk, Arundel Castle. GW.

14 Stone panel of Artillery at Edinburgh Castle, thought to date from the late sixteenth century. Phillipa Stirling-Langley.

15 Mons Meg. GW.

16 Norham Castle. NB.

17 Etal Castle. NB.

18 Portrait of James IV, by Daniel Mytens. In a private Scottish Collection, courtesy of the Scottish National Portrait Gallery.

19 Soldiers of Flodden, Richard Scollins, courtesy of Keith Durham.

20 Scottish heraldry at Flodden. GW.

21 English heraldry. GW.

22 The 'Flodden Archers' window, St Leonard's Church, Middleton, Lancs., courtesy of the Parochial Parish Council of St Leonards and Canon Nicholas Feist.

23 Drawing of Sir Ralph Assheton and wife (1845). GW.

24 This coloured engraving of 1845 shows a detail from the complete window. GW.

25 Tomb of John, Lord Sempill at the Collegiate Church of Castle Semple, Lochwinnoch. Richard Pearson.

26 Memorial brass epitaph to Sir Marmaduke Constable, St Oswald's Church, Flamborough, Yorkshire. GW.

27 *The Death of King James IV*. Richard Scollins, courtesy of Keith Durham.

28 *News of Flodden* by William Hole (1902) showing the 'Blew Blanket' banner. GW.

29 The 'Truth Prevails', bloodstained standard of William Keith, Earl Marischal of Scotland, by courtesy of the Faculty of Advocates, Edinburgh.

30 Engraving of the 'Blew Blanket, or 'Craftsman's Banner'. GW.

31 Artist's impression of the turquoise ring sent by the queen of France to James IV. GW.

32 Paxton House Banner Fragment, by courtesy of the Paxton Trust.

33 Illuminated copy of the Flodden List, St Oswald's Church, Arncliffe, Yorks. J.L. Kendall.

34 Portrait of Thomas Howard, 3rd Duke of Norfolk. GW.

35 Twizzell Bridge. NB.

36 Memorial brass to Sir William Molyneux and wives, Sefton, Lancs. GW.

37 Panoramic photograph of Branxton village. NB.

38 Branxton Hill from the English ridge. NB.

39 The area of Home and Huntly's advance at the western edge of Branxton Hill. NB.

40 The stream at the bottom of Branxton Hill. NB.

41 Effigies of Sir Richard Cholmondeley and his wife. St Peter Ad Vincula, Tower of London. GW.

42 James IV's sword and dagger, now in the College of Arms, London. GW.

43 Branxton Church. NB.

44 The remains of the Collegiate Church, Castle Semple, Lochwinnoch, Renfrew. Richard Pearson.

45 The Howard Augmentation on the Fitzroy tomb at Framlingham, Suffolk. GW.

46 Howard shield with the Flodden Augmentation in glass, Barham Hall. GW.

47 Flodden Wall at Edinburgh. Philippa Stirling-Langley.

48 The Selkirk statue of Fletcher by Thomas Clapperton, Halliwell's House Museum, Selkirk.

INDEX